Breathing Disorders

Your *Complete Exercise* *Guide*

The Cooper Clinic and Research Institute Fitness Series

Neil F. Gordon, MD, PhD, MPH
The Cooper Institute for Aerobics Research
Dallas, Texas

Huers

To Shirley, Richard, and Nadine—with love
Neil F. Gordon, MD, PhD, MPH

Library of Congress Cataloging-in-Publication Data

Gordon, Neil F.
  Breathing disorders : your complete exercise guide / Neil F.
Gordon.
    p. cm. -- (The Cooper Clinic and Research Institute fitness
series)
  Includes bibliographical references and index.
  ISBN 0-87322-426-4
  1. Respiratory organs--Diseases--Exercise therapy. 2. Breathing
exercises. I. Title. II. Series.
RC735.E95G67 1993
616.2'062--dc20   92-42116
                                                       CIP

ISBN: 0-87322-426-4

Notice: Exercise and health are matters that vary necessarily between individuals. Readers should speak with their own doctors about their individual needs *before* starting any exercise program. This book is *not* intended as a substitute for the medical advice and supervision of your personal physician. Any application of the recommendations set forth in the following pages is at the reader's discretion and sole risk.

Human Kinetics books are available at special discounts for bulk purchase for sales promotions, premiums, fund-raising, or educational use. Special editions or book excerpts can also be created to specification. For details, contact the Special Sales Manager at Human Kinetics.

Printed in the United States of America   10 9 8 7 6 5 4 3 2 1

Human Kinetics Publishers
Box 5076, Champaign, IL 61825-5076
1-800-747-4457

Canada: Human Kinetics Publishers, P.O. Box 2503, Windsor, ON N8Y 4S2
1-800-465-7301 (in Canada only)

Europe: Human Kinetics Publishers (Europe) Ltd., P.O. Box IW14,
Leeds LS16 6TR, England   0532-781708

Australia: Human Kinetics Publishers, P.O. Box 80, Kingswood 5062,
South Australia   618-374-0433

New Zealand: Human Kinetics Publishers, P.O. Box 105-231,
Auckland 1   (09) 309-2259

Contents

Foreword

Each book in The Cooper Clinic and Research Institute Fitness Series covers an exercise rehabilitation program we devised to help our patients and others around the world recover from a chronic medical disorder. The series covers diabetes, chronic fatigue, stroke, arthritis, and breathing disorders.

I anticipate that the readers of this book will be highly motivated fighters—people who aren't going to let their respiratory ailment get the best of them. They're going to do what needs to be done to fight back and grow healthier through exercise, despite the fact that their breathing disorders may be chronic. If you've got perseverance and you're determined to feel better, you've got the right book in your hands. For I believe my staff at The Cooper Aerobics Center* and I have developed one of America's finest and safest exercise rehabilitation programs for people with your medical problem.

*The Cooper Aerobics Center, founded by Ken Cooper in Dallas in the early 1970s, is comprised of the Cooper Clinic, a preventive and rehabilitative medicine facility; The Cooper Institute for Aerobics Research, where researchers study the role of exercise and other lifestyle factors in the maintenance of health; the Cooper Wellness Program, which provides a supportive, live-in environment where participants can focus time and attention on the challenging task of how to make positive lifestyle changes; and the Cooper Fitness Center, a health club in which all members' exercise efforts are supervised by a well-trained staff of health professionals.

With all the controversy and publicity over the hazards of smoking, lung diseases have been in the limelight over the past couple of decades—for good reason. It's a sad fact that although mortality rates for the other leading causes of death in the United States, such as heart disease, have been declining steadily, mortality rates for lung cancer and *chronic obstructive pulmonary diseases* (COPD) have been increasing.[1] Between 1966 and 1986, COPD deaths alone increased 71%.

The statistics on COPD, the cluster of respiratory ailments we focus on in this book, are startling. COPD is the direct cause or a leading contributing factor in about 8.3% of deaths in the United States each year—some 170,000 fatalities.[2] The numbers of people affected by various COPDs are even bigger. Almost 10 million people in the United States have asthma, more than 11 million have chronic bronchitis, and 2 million have emphysema.[2]

One of the worst things about respiratory ailments is how they affect people's lives. Even a moderate breathing problem can impair a person's ability to be a productive and fully functional member of society. Fortunately, appropriate exercise can do a lot to reverse COPD's debilitating symptoms, the worst of which is periodic, maybe even constant, breathlessness. It's because rehabilitative exercise as an alleviator of such symptoms is not emphasized enough in the pulmonary treatment books already on the market that we felt it necessary to write this one. What this book offers that others don't is comprehensive, state-of-the-art advice on how a breathing disorder patient should go about starting an exercise program, including information about just how much and what kind of exercise will improve your health.

Readers familiar with my books know that I believe people need all the motivation they can get to break a bad health habit and replace it with a good one. To provide you with a strong incentive to maintain your health through regular exertion while at the same time avoiding the aspects of exercise that are risky for breathing disorder patients, this book comes complete with a Health Points System. It's a great system designed to keep you exercising over the long haul. It will ease you into a healthier lifestyle and motivate you to keep going, even on those days when you feel most tempted to backslide.

It's my hope that this book will serve as a springboard for discussions about exercise between you and your doctor. I also hope it will make you more self-sufficient and less dependent on your physician for all the details on how to work exercise into your daily routine. On the other hand, I don't ever want you to regard our advice as a substitute for that of your doctor or any other health-care practitioner familiar with your case.

Pulmonary rehabilitation has come a long way over the years. Today, breathing disorder patients can be given the tools—one of which is exercise—to exert more control over their problem than ever before. As you read this book, many of you will discover you can partially—or almost fully—reverse the disability and loss of functional capacity that your disorder has caused. Yes, it's likely you can return to a more active lifestyle.

Kenneth H. Cooper, MD, MPH

About the Author

D r. Neil F. Gordon is widely regarded as a leading medical authority on exercise and health. Before receiving his master's degree in public health from the University of California at Los Angeles in 1989, Dr. Gordon received doctoral degrees in exercise physiology and medicine at the University of the Witwatersrand in Johannesburg, South Africa. He also served as medical director of cardiac rehabilitation and exercise physiology for 6 years at I Military Hospital in Pretoria, South Africa.

Since 1987, Dr. Gordon has been the director of exercise physiology at the internationally renowned Cooper Institute for Aerobics Research in Dallas, Texas. He has also written over 50 papers on exercise and medicine.

Dr. Gordon is a member of the American Heart Association and American Diabetes Association. He is a fellow of the American College of Sports Medicine and the American Association of Cardiovascular and Pulmonary Rehabilitation (AACVPR). He also has served on the board of directors for AACVPR, the Texas Association of Cardiovascular and Pulmonary Rehabilitation, and the American Heart Association (Dallas affiliate).

Preface

Any series of books as comprehensive as The Cooper Clinic and Research Institute Fitness Series is likely to have an interesting story behind it, and this one certainly does. The story began over a decade ago, shortly after I completed my medical training. Because of my keen interest in sports medicine (which was why I went to medical school in the first place) I volunteered to help establish an exercise rehabilitation program for patients with chronic diseases at a major South African hospital. To get the ball rolling I decided to telephone patients who had recently been treated at the hospital. My very first call planted the seed for writing a series of books that would educate patients with chronic medical conditions about the many benefits of a physically active lifestyle and lead them step-by-step down the road to improved health.

That telephone call was an eye-opener for me, a relative novice in the field of rehabilitation medicine. The patient, a middle-aged man who had recently suffered a heart attack, bellowed into the phone: "Why are you trying to create more problems for me? Isn't it enough that I've been turned into an invalid for the rest of my life by a heart attack?" Fortunately I kept my cool and convinced him to give the program a try—after all, what did he have to lose? Within months he was "miraculously" transformed into a man with a new zest for life. Like the thousands of men and women with chronic disorders with whom I've subsequently worked with in South Africa and, more recently, the United States, he had experienced the numerous physical and psychological benefits of a medically prescribed exercise rehabilitation program.

Today, it's known that a comprehensive exercise rehabilitation program, such as the one outlined in this book, is an essential component of state-of-the-art medical care for patients with a variety of chronic conditions. But, despite the many benefits that have continued to unfold through research, patients with chronic medical conditions are usually not much better informed than the previously mentioned patient was prior to my telephone call. This book is meant to help fill this void for persons with breathing disorders such as chronic bronchitis, emphysema, and asthma, by providing you with practical, easy-to-follow information about exercise rehabilitation for use in collaboration with your doctor.

To accomplish this, I've set out this book as follows. In chapter 1 you'll meet two of our breathing disorder patients, whose stories will introduce you to some basic concepts about respiratory problems, exercise, and rehabilitation. In chapter 2 you'll discover the wonderful benefits of a physically active lifestyle. Toward the end of this chapter, however, I try to temper my obvious enthusiasm for exercise by pointing out some of its potential risks for persons with breathing disorders. In chapter 3 I'll show you step-by-step how to begin a sensible exercise rehabilitation program. In chapter 4 you'll learn how to use the Health Points System to determine precisely how much exercise you need to do to optimize your health and fitness, without exerting yourself to the point where exercise can become risky. At the end of this chapter, I'll give you some useful tips for sticking with your exercise program once you get started. Finally, in chapter 5 I'll provide you with essential safety guidelines. Although exercise is a far more normal state for the human body than being sedentary, I want you to keep your risk, however small it may be, as low as possible.

View the programs in this book as prototypes. It is up to you and your doctor to make changes in these prototypes—that is, to adapt my programs—to suit the medical realities of your specific respiratory ailment. Set realistic goals for yourself. Above all, remember that no book can remove the need for close supervision by a patient's own doctor.

By the time you have completed this book, I hope that you'll have renewed hope for a healthier, longer, more enjoyable life. If you then act on the advice and adopt a more physically active lifestyle, the time spent preparing *Breathing Disorders: Your Complete Exercise Guide* will have been well worth the effort.

Neil F. Gordon, MD, PhD, MPH

Acknowledgments

To prepare a series of books as comprehensive and complex as this, I have required the assistance and cooperation of many talented people. To adequately acknowledge all would be impossible. However, I would be remiss not to recognize a few special contributions.

Ken Cooper, MD, MPH, chairman and founder of the Cooper Clinic, was of immense assistance in initiating this series. In addition to writing the foreword and providing many useful suggestions, he continues to serve as an inspiration to me and millions of people around the world.

Larry Gibbons, MD, MPH, medical director of the Cooper Clinic, coauthored with me *The Cooper Clinic Cardiac Rehabilitation Program*. In doing so, he made an invaluable contribution to many of the concepts used in this series, especially the Health Points System.

Jacqueline Thompson, a talented writer based in Staten Island, New York, provided excellent editorial assistance with the first draft of this series. Her contributions and those of Herb Katz, a New York–based literary agent, greatly enhanced the practical value of this series.

Charles Sterling, EdD, executive director of The Cooper Institute for Aerobics Research, provided much needed guidance and support while working on this series, as did John Duncan, PhD; Chris Scott, MS; Pat Brill, PhD; Kia Vaandrager, MS; Conrad Earnest, MS; Sheila

Burford, and my many other colleagues at the Institute, Cooper Clinic, Cooper Wellness Program, and Cooper Fitness Center.

Michael Belman, MD, a world-renowned pulmonologist from Cedars-Sinai Medical Center, Los Angeles, reviewed the first draft of *Breathing Disorders: Your Complete Exercise Guide* and provided many excellent suggestions.

My thanks to Rainer Martens, president of Human Kinetics Publishers, without whom this series could not have been published. Rainer, Holly Gilly (my developmental editor), and other staff members at Human Kinetics Publishers did a fantastic job in making this series a reality. It was a pleasure and gratifying experience to work with them.

A special thanks to the patients who allowed me to tell their stories and to all my patients over the years from whom I have learned so much about exercise and rehabilitation.

Finally, I want to thank my wonderful family—my wife, Tracey, and daughters, Kim and Terri—for their patience, support, and understanding in preparing this series.

To these people and the many others far too numerous to list, many thanks for making this book a reality, and in so doing benefiting patients with respiratory ailments around the world.

Credits

Developmental Editor—Holly Gilly; *Assistant Editors*—Valerie Hall, Dawn Roselund; *Copyeditor*—Jane Bowers; *Proofreader*—Christine Drews; *Indexer*—Theresa Schaefer; *Production Director*—Ernie Noa; *Text Design*—Keith Blomberg; *Text Layout*—Sandra Meier, Tara Welsch; *Cover Design*—Jack Davis; *Factoids*—Doug Burnett; *Technique Drawings*—Tim Offenstein; *Interior Art*—Kathy Fuoss, Gretchen Walters; *Printer*—United Graphics

The Cooper Clinic and Research Institute Fitness Series

Arthritis: *Your Complete Exercise Guide*

Breathing Disorders: *Your Complete Exercise Guide*

Chronic Fatigue: *Your Complete Exercise Guide*

Diabetes: *Your Complete Exercise Guide*

Stroke: *Your Complete Exercise Guide*

Chapter 1

Learning to Breathe Again

As a medical doctor and exercise physiologist, and as a jogger, I've thought a lot about breathing over the years. Deep breathing, after all, is central to exercise. Long before I became interested in breathing from a professional viewpoint, I learned first-hand just how crucial—and beneficial—aerobic exercise can be for someone with a breathing disorder.

Years ago, as a high school student in South Africa, I was a serious middle-distance track athlete. I set a record for the 800 meters that stood for almost 10 years. My biggest competitor, a fellow named Jeff Malin, had chronic asthmatic bronchitis. Just before each race, he used an inhaler containing medication to unblock his bronchial tubes. Jeff was such a remarkable performer despite his condition that he became a national-class marathon runner. (I once tried using his inhaler before a race under the mistaken belief it could help me, too. But all it did was speed up my heart rate and make me feel jittery.)

What did aerobic exercise do for Jeff? It transformed him from a shy, hesitant teenage boy into a high school hero. It also made him healthier and less in need of emergency visits to the hospital for resuscitation after his bouts with asthma.

Jeff is no oddball example of athletic perseverance in the face of a breathing disorder. Of the 667 U.S. team members at the 1988 Olympic Games in Seoul, South Korea, 52 had confirmed exercise-induced asthma and another 50 were suspected to have it. And surprisingly, the same percentage of athletes with this malady won medals as did those without it.[1]

Jackie Joyner-Kersee, a track-and-field silver medalist at the 1984 Olympic Games in Los Angeles, two-time gold medalist at the 1988 Olympics in Seoul, and gold medalist at the 1992 Olympics in Barcelona, learned she had a breathing problem in 1983. A colleague with the same condition insisted she see an allergist for her persistent wheezing. The doctor did some tests and diagnosed asthma. He prescribed medications and suggested some changes in her training regimen in line with the maxim "Work with your condition—not against it."

In this book, I'll teach you how to work with your condition to reduce your breathlessness through specific types of exercises. These exercises will also foster your long-term health and fitness.

Many world-class athletes have breathing disorders and have overcome obstacles similar to those facing some of you. These athletes include Bill Koch, one of America's top cross-country ski racers; Karin Smith, a four-time Olympian in the javelin throw; Danny Manning, the 1987-88 College Basketball Player of the Year; and Nancy Hogshead, the swimmer who won three gold medals and one silver at the 1984 Olympics. Aerobic conditioning has made their bodies use oxygen more efficiently: Their hearts can pump more oxygen-rich blood with less effort, and their muscles need less oxygen to do the same amount of work.

The exercise program outlined in this book is designed to do exciting things for you as well. I don't expect you to become a competitive athlete, but there's no reason you shouldn't realize, albeit to a lesser degree, the same wonderful benefits as these celebrity athletes have from regular, endurance-oriented exercise. Ordinary people are learning to do just that every day at The Cooper Aerobics Center, as the following two case histories demonstrate.

CASE HISTORY OF DAVE SAXON

Dave Saxon, who is 66 years old, is typical of his generation. He and his peers began smoking as young adults; back then, society gave the practice a green light, so many people smoked with impunity. Dave began smoking as a serviceman in Europe during the Second World War.

For years, Dave had "smoker's cough"—a cough that often brought up sputum—but no other symptoms. About 5 years ago, things changed. He noticed that walking up a flight of stairs or similar exertion made him more out of breath than usual. And during the winter he developed a chest infection that got so serious he had to be admitted to the hospital for intravenous antibiotic therapy. When the infection was under control, his doctor put him through a series of pulmonary function tests. The diagnosis was chronic bronchitis, which, his physician warned, could worsen if Dave didn't quit smoking immediately.

Like a lot of people, Dave ignored the warning. Sure enough, his cough and exertional breathlessness got progressively worse, even though Dave was using the oral and inhaler medications his doctor had prescribed. Dave found a cure for one of his symptoms, though. He stopped doing any activity that made him out of breath, which meant zero exercise from then on. Dave hadn't participated in sports or formal exercise for years anyway, so he found it no great loss. But he found it annoying not to be able to walk fast or hurry to catch a bus.

Over a year's time, Dave's condition worsened. At his wife's insistence, he went for a checkup. His doctor warned that if Dave continued to smoke, his condition could evolve into emphysema. This time it took little coaxing to motivate Dave to think seriously about when and how to quit.

Dave entered a smoking-cessation program that also had a component for reteaching heavy smokers how to breathe correctly. Dave was an apt pupil. Next, his doctor referred him to The Cooper Aerobics Center for exercise rehabilitation in our 12-week medically supervised workout program.

To obtain a benchmark reading of his fitness level and maximum heart rate, Dave underwent a treadmill exercise test. The results weren't good, but that was no surprise to anyone. In the early stages of the program, Dave followed a daily routine of flexibility exercises, muscle strengthening with light, hand-held weights, and easy aerobic exercise consisting of 5 minutes each of slow walking and stationary cycling. By the end of 3 months, Dave was doing the same stretching routine, but he used heavier weights for muscle strengthening, and he'd progressed to about 20 minutes each of walking and cycling on a bike that worked his arms and legs simultaneously. However, Dave continued to have frequent shortness of breath, so I suggested he try *interval training.* If aerobics made Dave unduly tired, he could slow down for a while until he got a second wind—or, if really necessary, stop until he felt able to continue.

A year has passed, and Dave looks and feels like a new man. The numbers tell the tale. His strength, measured by the amount of weight he uses on our resistance-training machines and equipment at the Cooper Fitness Center, has increased by 40%. His aerobic fitness, as indicated by his endurance during a second treadmill exercise test, has increased by almost 30%. He credits the Health Points System, which I'll describe in chapter 4, as leading the way. He says it was an especially critical motivator during periods when he lost his resolve and was tempted to slack off. Most weeks Dave earns between 50 and 100 health points, the amount I recommend.

Today, Dave has far less breathlessness during his everyday life despite the fact that his pulmonary function tests haven't improved. This is to be expected, because the underlying disease and the damage it has caused cannot be reversed, even though the symptoms often can be greatly alleviated. Dave coughs less and happily reports he has had no serious chest infections during the year he's been exercising

Case history, Dave Saxon

Patient Name: Dave Saxon
Occupation: Commodities Buyer

Complaint: Smoker's cough, chest infection, exertional breathlessness
Diagnosis: Chronic bronchitis developing into emphysema
Prescription: Exercise, don't smoke, breathe properly, use medications

with us. And because of both exercise and an improved diet, his blood-lipid profile is in better balance, indicating a lessened risk for developing heart disease. This is important to Dave because his father died of it at a rather young age. Dave sleeps better, has fewer bouts of anxiety and depression, and has an improved self-image. His wife is particularly pleased with his progress because Dave now has enough wind in his sails to take her dancing again.

CASE HISTORY OF JOYCE TRYGSTAD

If Dave Saxon's story wasn't enough to blunt your skepticism about exercise, let me introduce you to another of our Cooper Aerobics Center regulars. Joyce Trygstad, a professional woman and Cooper Clinic patient, was a young adult when she developed chronic asthmatic bronchitis.[2] Her condition was so bad that she lost a year of graduate school because she couldn't walk the five blocks to class every day. Finally, she found relief with an inhaled steroid and exercise, which she says helped enormously.

Case history, Joyce Trygstad

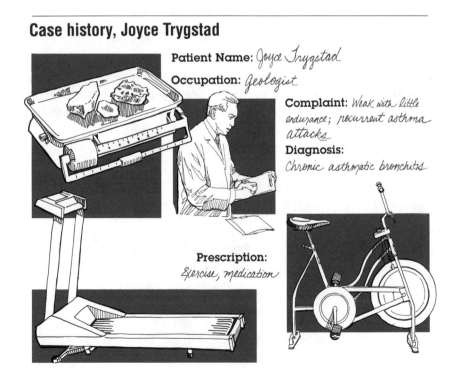

Patient Name: Joyce Trygstad
Occupation: Geologist
Complaint: Weak with little endurance; recurrent asthma attacks
Diagnosis: Chronic asthmatic bronchitis
Prescription: Exercise, medication

Joyce, like Dave, started out in the 12-week supervised rehabilitation course because, after avoiding sports for many years due to her ailment, she was weak and had little endurance. But that changed dramatically and quickly. Not long after completing the program and continuing with regular exercise training, Joyce had improved enough to risk a 2-week hiking adventure in the Colorado Rockies.

"We spent all our time above 9,000 feet, averaging 6 hours a day of hiking," Joyce recalls. "I was never tired or unusually short of breath. We even scaled Mount Sneffels [14,150 feet], and I felt *fantastic!*"

Since then, Joyce has remained faithful to a combination walking, swimming, and stretching program. She finds swimming particularly energizing because she says breathing moist, warm air helps prevent her air passages from blocking up.

Joyce says, "When I exercise regularly, I feel much better all over but especially in ease of breathing." Now when Joyce gets colds or flu-like symptoms, she says she doesn't worry as much that they'll immediately go to her chest and create complications—an important concern for anyone with a breathing disorder.[2]

WHAT CONSTITUTES
A BREATHING DISORDER?

Of course, it's normal to become short of breath when you engage in a strenuous activity. But becoming breathless under other circumstances usually is not normal. The following checklist lists conditions in which breathlessness generally is not normal. One or more of them may indicate there's some underlying disease causing your problem.

✓   Do You Have a Problem   ✓
With Breathlessness?

If any of the following are true, your breathlessness is probably caused by disease.

_____ I'm more breathless than other people my age when doing various physical activities.

_____ I get out of breath when doing things that only a few months ago didn't cause this reaction.

_____ I have sudden bouts of breathlessness when there's no apparent reason for it, like when I increase my exertion.

_____

Source: Adapted from K.M. Moser, C. Archibald, P. Hansen et al., _Shortness of Breath: A Guide to Better Living and Breathing._ St. Louis: C.V. Mosby Co., 1983.

Breathlessness is a symptom of a number of diseases, among them anemia, endocrine imbalances, and heart ailments, to name but a few. In this book, I'll focus on the most common cause of breathlessness—namely, disorders involving the lungs, your body's _pulmonary_, or breathing, apparatus (see Figure 1.1).

The main symptom of such breathing disorders is the sensation of not being able to take in enough air, a feeling of being out of breath or breathless. In his book about how he overcame his asthmatic condition and excelled as an operatic tenor and well-known actor, Paul Sorvino describes how breathlessness feels:

"Like you've just raced 50 yards at full speed, though all you've done is gotten up from your chair. You can't catch your breath, your chest is heaving, and you're coughing unproductively. . . . It can make life lose its naturalness, for you and for those around you. Understandably, it's tough for them to pretend everything is fine while you stand there gasping for air."[3]

This labored breathing, called _dyspnea_ (pronounced disp-nee-ah), is actually a cluster of sensations that each patient describes a little differently.[4] I know because I've had many patients with breathing disorders, and seldom are their complaints identical. I've noticed one thing, though. During the initial consultation, patients' explanations usually hint at the same underlying emotion: sheer panic at the idea they may one day become so out of breath that they'll suffocate. It's a common worry; that's why it takes a determined patient with a helpful doctor to brave the unknowns of exercise. After all, even healthy people breathe much more heavily when exercising.

Although I cannot claim that exercise is a remedy for all breathing disorders, some types of disorders and degrees of breathlessness can be helped enormously by a well-designed, targeted exercise program. And I'll discuss them in this book. But let me reassure you that you are unlikely to be putting your very life in jeopardy by following a sensible exercise program. In the remainder of this chapter and in the next, I'll discuss the benefits and risks of exercise for people with breathing disorders. You may be apprehensive now about exertion,

The lungs, in concert with the heart and bloodstream, supply the body with its primary energy source: oxygen. When we breathe in through our nose or mouth, oxygen-rich air travels down through the windpipe into the lungs. The windpipe, like the trunk of a tree, subdivides numerous times in a branchlike fashion. When it reaches the chest, it breaks into two bronchi, one reaching into each lung, and further into many smaller bronchial tubes in the lungs. The bronchial tubes culminate in leaflike clusters of tiny, elastic air sacs lined with blood vessels. These air sacs release life-sustaining oxygen into the blood and remove the deadly waste gas carbon dioxide from it.

The muscular walls of the larger air passageways are reinforced with cartilage to keep them from collapsing during breathing; cartilage, however, is completely absent from the smallest bronchial tubes. The entire air passageway is lined with mucus-producing cells, which keep the inner walls moist and trap any small foreign matter before it reaches the vital air sacs.

The 300 million or so air sacs in the lungs expand and contract the way balloons do. Because of their elasticity, we normally need to work only the respiratory muscles of our chest and abdomen (such as the diaphragm) to expand our lungs during inhalation. An elastic recoil mechanism gives the lungs the ability to snap back and expel gas automatically during exhalation. However, things change during exertion, when the body's need for oxygen increases substantially. Then we need to work our respiratory muscles both to inhale *and* exhale, a form of labored breathing that resembles what people with chronic obstructive pulmonary disorders (COPD) experience a good deal of the time.

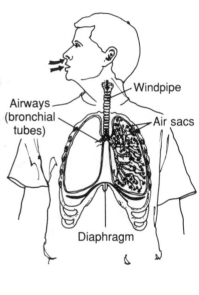

Airways (bronchial tubes)

Windpipe

Air sacs

Diaphragm

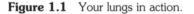

Figure 1.1 Your lungs in action.

but by the end of chapter 2, I think you'll feel exhilaration and anticipation instead. But first, here's a review of what your problem may be all about.

By far the most common of the problems affecting people's lungs—that delicate spongy tissue inside your chest—are the *obstructive lung diseases*. They're the ones I primarily feature in this book (for a description, see Table 1.1). Obstructive lung diseases make it difficult for those affected to expel air from their lungs, although each does so for slightly different reasons. The major symptoms, however, are the same: breathlessness, wheezing, and coughing.

Table 1.1
Glossary of Obstructive Breathing Disorders

Although there are people who have only one of the disorders below, many have a combination of them—sometimes because people tend to wait too long before seeking medical help (these disorders can be diagnosed via a physical exam, chest X rays, and pulmonary function tests). By the time some people are finally treated, the lung damage is often extensive and largely irreversible.

Episodic (or intermittent) asthma†

Symptoms	Sudden, usually short-lived attacks of wheezing on exhalation; breathlessness; sometimes coughing. No symptoms between attacks.
Triggers	Environmental pollutants; allergies to airborne substances or food; exposure to cold, dry air; extreme climatic changes; emotional stress; aspirin and other medications; respiratory infections such as colds; exercise.
Lung dysfunction	Bronchospasm (a narrowing of the bronchial tubes due to a sudden involuntary contraction of their walls); some inflammation of the lining of the bronchial tubes during attacks.
Response to therapy	Complete reversibility possible. For those with asthma caused by triggers, avoid the triggers. For those with asthma not caused by specific triggers, use medication.

Chronic asthmatic bronchitis*

Symptoms	Frequent, recurrent asthma attacks characterized by wheezing, varying degrees of breathlessness, and coughing.
Triggers	Same as for episodic asthma.
Lung dysfunction	Bronchospasm; thickening and inflammation of the walls of the bronchial tubes; some airflow obstruction between attacks.
Response to therapy	Partial reversibility of airflow obstruction and symptoms possible with medical therapy.

Chronic bronchitis*

Symptoms	Chronic daily cough that brings up sputum for at least 3 months per year for 2 consecutive years; accompanied by breathlessness and wheezing.
Triggers	Cigarette smoking.
Lung dysfunction	Inflammation of the bronchial tubes; excess mucous secretions; bronchospasm.
Response to therapy	Partial reversibility of airflow obstruction and symptoms possible with medical therapy.

Emphysema*

Symptoms	Breathlessness; coughing; wheezing.

(Cont.)

Table 1.1
(Continued)

Triggers	Cigarette smoking (major cause), which inhibits the action of protective enzymes in the lungs; inherited deficiency of protective enzymes (for nonsmokers).
Lung dysfunction	Air sac walls lose elasticity and ability to expel air from the lungs, which results in lungs remaining overinflated; air sac damage impedes gas exchange between lungs and bloodstream.
Response to therapy	Irreversible, but medical treatment can help relieve symptoms.

†A form of *obstructive lung disease*. Such disorders make it difficult to exhale air from the lungs.

*A subset of obstructive lung disease that is chronic—hence the term *chronic obstructive pulmonary disease* (COPD).

Except for *episodic asthma*, which can be treated so effectively that symptoms completely disappear, the remaining three disorders in the table are chronic: Some degree of obstruction to the outflow of air from the lungs (referred to as *airflow obstruction*) is always present. As Table 1.1 indicates, chronic asthmatic bronchitis, chronic bronchitis, and emphysema all fall under the rubric *chronic obstructive pulmonary disease* (COPD). Although I provide much useful information for those who experience episodic asthma, my book is likely to most benefit COPD patients.

No form of COPD is benign, but emphysema is the most deadly. Whereas only 15% of those with chronic asthmatic bronchitis are likely to die from it, or from complications arising from it, nearly 60% of emphysema patients die within 10 years of diagnosis.[5]

Naturally, any airflow obstruction is going to make the heavy breathing that exercise induces problematic. That's why people with breathing disorders should not take up exercise without thinking about the precautions needed. Yes, it's likely you can exercise. But if you have COPD, you cannot necessarily do every form of exercise, and the conditions under which you exercise must be carefully controlled.

COPD TREATMENT AND REHABILITATION

The first step in controlling COPD is to remove any factors that may trigger or worsen it. The following list outlines the major factors that predispose a person to COPD—and that may worsen it once they already have it. Some are within your control, like smoking and the pollutants you're exposed to in your neighborhood or at work. Others are beyond your control, such as your sex, age, and any genetic factors.

Unfortunately, by the time people make it to a doctor's office to review their symptoms, their lung damage is frequently beyond significant repair. So physicians tend to have a rather fatalistic attitude toward COPD patients. Instead of suggesting options like the one I outline in this book, which requires close monitoring, they often simply write out a prescription for a drug to relieve some of the symptoms and give a shrug that as much as says, "I give up. I can't do anything more."[6]

MAJOR RISK FACTORS FOR COPD

Risk factors are conditions that, collectively, predispose a person to a disease.

- Age. As you get older, your risk increases.
- Gender. Men are at somewhat greater risk than women.
- Cigarette smoking.
- Reduced lung function, even in the absence of any obvious symptoms.
- Occupational exposure to various pollutants, such as dusts and fumes.
- Air pollution.
- Acute respiratory tract infections, such as pneumonia and bronchitis.
- Episodic asthma. People with this condition are at increased risk for COPD.
- Deficiency (or lack) of alpha$_1$-antitrypsin. This is an inherited deficiency of an enzyme that normally protects the lungs from inflammatory damage. People who lack the enzyme may get emphysema at a rather young age, even if they don't smoke.

Source: Adapted from M. Higgins, "Epidemiology of COPD: State of the Art." *Chest*, 85 (1984): 3S-8S. Also, J.F. Murray (ed.), "Chronic Airways Disease—Distribution and Determinants, Prevention and Control." *Chest*, 96 (1989): 301S-378S.

COPD cannot be permanently cured, but medical science has progressed to where breathing disorder symptoms can often be alleviated to a great extent, thereby improving the patient's quality of life, and the risk for premature death can sometimes be reduced. The experts emphasize that pulmonary rehabilitation is the key to turning a negative outcome into a more positive one.[6,7]

If ever a form of rehabilitation was not cut-and-dried, it's pulmonary rehabilitation.[7] It requires a multidisciplinary approach in which patient education is crucial. When your condition was first diagnosed, your doctor should have fully explained the origins and evolution of your disease and prescribed appropriate medications. Those fortunate COPD patients with access to a broad range of treatment options would also have been helped by one or more of the following at various times during their rehabilitation:[8,9]

• *Physical therapists.* They teach bronchial drainage techniques, including how to cough effectively; deep-breathing techniques such as the pursed-lip maneuver; and relaxation techniques to relieve the stress of dealing with a chronic ailment.

• *Exercise physiologists.* Their goal—and mine in this book—is to use exercise as a means to help reduce breathlessness and improve overall functional capacity and mental outlook. Exercise has another, more long-term goal: to lessen the chances that you'll develop chronic ailments to which a sedentary lifestyle is an important contributing factor.

• *Occupational therapists.* They find ways to work around physical disabilities to make everyday life easier and to make patients better able to cope with their disabilities and function independently.

• *Respiratory therapists.* They teach you how to use supplemental oxygen and aerosol medications, if needed.

If you smoke, make enrollment in a smoking-cessation course a top priority. Get immunized regularly against influenza and pneumonia to help guard against illnesses that can easily cause major chest congestion. Also, be aware of the dangers of dehydration, which appears to cause a thickening of mucous secretions in the lungs. By all means, learn how to prevent this hazard. Finally, learn as much as possible about how environmental factors—such as temperature, humidity, altitude, and inhaled irritants—affect your condition. You need to know this so you can make changes to accommodate your body's special needs.

COPD rehab team

Exercise physiologist

Respiratory therapist

Physical therapist

Occupational therapist

Chronic labored breathing can destroy a person's confidence and ability to be the captain of his or her own life and destiny. Thus, treating this one symptom is a priority. The exercise program I present in this book will force your body to process oxygen more efficiently and will reduce the degree of breathlessness you experience during physical activity. It will also benefit you in many other ways, as you'll soon learn.

Chapter 2

Benefits and Risks of Exercise to Help Your Breathing Problems

If you're like most COPD patients, you waited too long before you consulted a doctor about your condition, got drug treatment, and entered a pulmonary rehabilitation program. By the time you did, you probably were already enmeshed in what's known as a *disability spiral*.[1] This means you reacted to your disease by adopting a way of life that played down your major symptom: breathlessness. You did as little physical exertion as possible and no formal exercise. In doing this, you ignored the long-term implications of a sedentary lifestyle. Unfortunately, this approach to living is guaranteed to foster more disability, not less.

Back in the fifth century B.C., the Greek physician Hippocrates recognized that this approach was foolhardy and dangerous over time. Hippocrates wrote, "All parts of the body which have a function, if used in moderation and exercised in labours in which each is accustomed, become thereby healthy, well-developed and age more slowly. But if unused and left idle, they become liable to disease, defective in growth, and age quickly."[2] Essentially, it's the principle implied in the popular saying "Use it or lose it."

But ancient physicians also realized that breathing problems can make certain kinds of exercise difficult. By the second century A.D., the term *asthma* was appearing in the medical literature. Aretaeus the Cappadocian wrote, "If from running, gymnastic exercises, or any other work, the breathing becomes difficult, it is called Asthma."[3]

Today, by taking appropriate medical treatment and following special safety guidelines, people with episodic asthma or COPD can exercise and realize vital, life-sustaining benefits. In the short term, exercise can yield a higher level of fitness and energy and a renewed sense of well-being. Longer term advantages include a lower risk of developing chronic ailments such as heart disease, diabetes, high blood pressure, osteoporosis, and possibly certain types of cancer and stroke. Believe me, the benefits of regular exercise are so numerous that describing them could take up the entire book![4]

Exercise is a good health habit. No doctor and few laypeople today would dispute this. Nor is there anything controversial about including exercise in pulmonary rehabilitation programs. In the early 1960s, doctors began prescribing exercise as they do drugs—first, to *prevent* sickness and then, after the fact, to *rehabilitate* patients with specific chronic illnesses. Lung diseases are high on the list of conditions for which exercise is deemed an appropriate, worthwhile therapy.

The question you should ask yourself about my exercise program is this: Is it safe and affordable, and will it help me live longer while reducing discomfort and disability? For most people with respiratory problems, the experts think judicious exercise as part of an overall pulmonary rehabilitation program fills this bill.[5-8] In this chapter I'll explain why.

RELIEVES DISCOMFORT AND REVERSES DISABILITY

No doubt the major discomfort you feel is breathlessness at inconvenient times—or, perhaps, breathlessness almost all the time. This unpleasant sensation is caused largely by airflow obstruction. You should see your doctor and, if necessary, get appropriate drug treatment to stabilize your chest condition, removing as much of the obstruction as possible, before you start exercising.[9] But be forewarned that COPD patients who do this find, to their chagrin, that even after they've been exercising for a while, their pulmonary function test results remain unchanged.

Upon reading this, you may ask, Why bother to exercise if it isn't going to improve my condition? The truth is exercise will reduce your breathlessness even though your pulmonary function tests won't show any improvement. This anomalous situation can be explained with a lesson in physiology. You may be surprised which bodily functions and systems grow stronger and healthier with regular exercise and which stay the same.

When a healthy person performs all-out exercise, the major factor that eventually causes exhaustion is not breathlessness but muscle fatigue. This may result because the heart and circulatory system cannot provide the working muscles with adequate oxygen-rich blood. It is not because of the lungs' inability to take in sufficient oxygen.[10]

Your situation may be somewhat different. When you first begin exercising, you may not reach the muscle-fatigue stage. Long before your muscles tire, you'll be gasping for air so much that you'll have to stop. However, if you proceed gradually with exercise, as I outline in this book, your endurance will grow and breathlessness will eventually become less of a problem. This won't be due to an improvement in the condition of your lungs. The reasons for such benefits can be better understood by considering a few more details about your lungs' reaction to exercise. (I'll refer to these concepts again in chapter 3.)

Lungs' Response to Exercise

The degree of your breathlessness during exercise depends on a delicate balance between your body's *ventilatory requirement* and its *ventilatory capacity*. The ventilatory requirement is how much air your lungs must breathe in and out during exercise to satisfy your body's need for oxygen and to expel carbon dioxide waste gas. Your ventilatory capacity is how much air you're, in fact, able to breathe in and out during exercise. This depends on the health of your lungs and is reduced in people with COPD. When your body's ventilatory requirement exceeds your lungs' ventilatory capacity (which COPD patients can expect to happen relatively quickly when they first begin to exercise), extreme breathlessness results, and you must stop and rest.[11] In short, your body needs you to breathe more air than your lungs are capable of doing (a problem that people with healthy lungs do not experience).

Depending on the disorder, a person with COPD may have one or more of the following adverse lung conditions (all of which reduce

Effects of exercise on diseased lungs

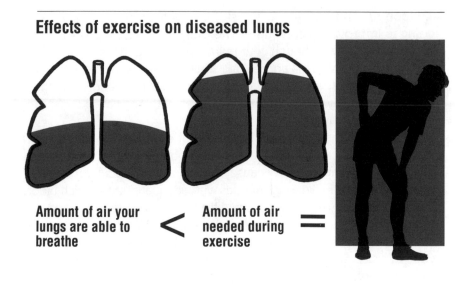

Amount of air your lungs are able to breathe < Amount of air needed during exercise =

When ventilatory capacity is less than ventilatory requirement, breathlessness results

ventilatory capacity or increase the ventilatory requirement during exertion, or both):

- Airflow is obstructed.
- The lung tissue has lost much of its vital ability to snap back after inhalation and expel air automatically, causing chronically inflated lungs.
- The air sacs in the lungs are inefficient at releasing oxygen into the blood and removing carbon dioxide from it (known as *impaired gas exchange*).

Unfortunately, regular exercise cannot reverse these conditions to any appreciable extent. But the more you persevere with exercise, the less you'll be bothered by breathlessness, because you'll realize improvements in some of the other factors that determine the body's ventilatory requirement. For example, you may reduce the amount of oxygen needed to perform a given amount of exercise, the amount of carbon dioxide produced during exercise, and the amount of lactic acid that your muscles produce during exercise.[12,13] (Lactic acid production by the muscles is often what makes healthy exercisers so fatigued they must stop; it also increases the ventilatory requirement.) These benefits result from the improved efficiency of your cardiovascular and musculoskeletal systems. Add to that the possible increases in the strength and endurance of the respiratory muscles in your chest and abdomen, and you should understand why I say,

Exercise, exercise, exercise—even if it doesn't improve your results on pulmonary function tests. Those results are beside the point, for all the reasons I have outlined.

Rating Functional Capacity

A COPD patient who has improved his or her exercise performance by 20% to 30%—an amount typical for my patients—goes about the tasks of daily living with more verve and less disability than before. Such a person has greater functional capacity and, as such, gets more joy out of life and is a more productive member of society.[14,15]

The degree of your disability due to breathlessness when you start your exercise program will affect your probable improvement and the precise health benefits you'll realize. Use the following box to grade the extent of your problem now, before you begin working out regularly.

BREATHLESSNESS DISABILITY SCALE

Grade 1 disability (none or almost none)	You become severely out of breath only when you're engaged in heavy exertion.
Grade 2 disability (mild)	You have to breathe harder than normal when walking on inclines or when you're hurrying on level ground.
Grade 3 disability (moderate)	You can still function adequately (walk a mile slowly, do your own shopping, etc.), but you cannot keep up with people of your age and physique during a stroll on level ground.
Grade 4 disability (severe)	Even the mildest exertion makes you out of breath. You cannot walk one city block or climb a flight of stairs without stopping to gasp for air.

Source: Adapted from Medical Research Council, Committee on Research into Chronic Bronchitis. *Instructions for the Use of the Questionnaire on Respiratory Symptoms.* Devon, England: W.J. Holman, 1966.

If you fall into Grade 1, you're in the same category as healthy people who exercise. You can expect, with exercise training, to improve your fitness level and to substantially reduce your risk for premature death from other chronic diseases—a benefit I'll discuss in more detail later.

In addition to these benefits, for those with a Grade 2, or mild, disability, exercise will also reduce that annoying exertional breathlessness and, thus, give you greater functional capacity.

Those with a Grade 3 disability will find it harder to lessen their risk of chronic disease or premature death, because exercise will be more challenging for them. Whether they'll be able to consistently earn the recommended 50 to 100 health points using the system described in chapter 4 is an individual matter. However, to the extent that they do persevere and exercise regularly each week, they'll notice a decisive turnabout in their breathlessness, which will seem all the more beneficial because their problem was greater to begin with.

Unfortunately, COPD patients with a Grade 4 disability are already so impaired that they may not be able to do enough exercise to substantially reduce their long-term risk. For these people, some relief from exertional dyspnea and a somewhat-improved functional capacity may be all they'll gain. Still, even this incremental improvement in one's condition will help improve the quality of life.

REDUCES YOUR CHANCES
OF DYING PREMATURELY
OR DEVELOPING OTHER DISEASES

How much your very survival is threatened by your respiratory condition depends on two things: the precise disease you have and the stage your problem had reached when you first began receiving medical treatment.

For example, a person whose emphysema was diagnosed late in its course is at the greatest risk of dying relatively soon, both from respiratory failure and from a special type of heart enlargement called *cor pulmonale*. (When the right side of the heart is forced to work harder to pump blood through diseased lungs, it sometimes becomes enlarged. This can lead to heart failure.)

Can a comprehensive pulmonary rehabilitation program that includes regular exercise make much difference when a person's situation is that serious? More research needs to be done to clarify this issue. For example, there's still no data on the impact of exercise on someone with cor pulmonale. But there is abundant evidence that regular exercise can help people with other forms of heart failure whose condition has been stabilized with drugs.[16]

Also, both anecdotal evidence and studies suggest that a good pulmonary rehabilitation program can help improve the lives of COPD patients and possibly their survival rates even for patients with advanced COPD. For example, physicians from the New York University Medical School studied several hundred patients with varying degrees of COPD, some of whom went through a special pulmonary rehabilitation program. The death rate among the patients who went through the rehabilitation program was reduced by a staggering 48% during the 5-year study.[14]

Unlike those with advanced COPD, people with chronic asthmatic bronchitis or chronic bronchitis who are diagnosed early have a relatively good prognosis. Like most people, they're probably more likely to die from coronary artery disease (the disease that causes heart attacks) than from their lung disorders.

In 1987, Kenneth E. Powell and his colleagues at the Centers for Disease Control reviewed more than 40 respected studies, some dating back to the 1950s. Their goal was to assess how, and if, exercise can prevent deaths from coronary artery disease in previously healthy people.[17] They concluded that physical *inactivity* is just as strong a risk factor for premature death from heart disease as the traditional risk factors you hear so much about—cigarette smoking, high blood pressure, and a high cholesterol level. Since Powell's overview was published, several other key studies have been done that strongly support the Powell group's conclusions. The evidence is compelling that regular exercise can reduce your chances—by almost 50%—of dying from coronary artery disease.[18]

So although you may not die from your COPD, it can ease you into a lifestyle that's lethal. People who use their respiratory ailments as an excuse to put their feet up and coddle themselves for the remainder of their days are likely to shorten those days considerably. Sitting around in an easy chair day-in-and-day-out is almost guaranteed to invite other ailments that are as devastating as your respiratory problem. That's why I'm urging you to get up, put on your sweats, and get going.

IMPROVES YOUR OUTLOOK
AND QUALITY OF LIFE

I'd be foolish to claim that regular exercise is a panacea for psychological problems, but I do know, from scientific as well as anecdotal evidence, that it can help profoundly. Several studies have shown that chronic disease patients who exercise faithfully have less stress, anxiety, and depression; sleep better; and have enhanced self-esteem. A consensus panel of the National Institute of Mental Health in the United States likewise maintains that exercise and physical fitness have a positive influence on most people's mental outlook and well-being, regardless of age. For depressed people, medical specialists now view regular exercise as a useful adjunct to medication or psychotherapy, or both.[19]

The American Association of Cardiovascular and Pulmonary Rehabilitation also singles out "improvement in psychological function with less anxiety and depression and increased feelings of hope, control and self-esteem" as a key benefit of a comprehensive pulmonary rehabilitation program, of which exercise is an important component.[5]

How can regular exercise enhance self-esteem? It's well known in the exercise community that 50% of people who start an aerobic exercise program drop out within 3 to 6 months. If you can defy this statistic, imagine how you'll feel. In effect, exercise will symbolize your perseverance, your ability to make a commitment and stick with it. Exercise will provide tangible proof that you have more control than you thought over your condition. This knowledge will help prevent a syndrome known as *learned helplessness*, in which patients come to believe their illness is totally beyond their control, to be borne with as much stoicism as possible. Learned helplessness results in a vicious downward spiral of further psychological problems and dependence on others. Taken to its logical conclusion, it results in invalidism.

Ken Cooper likes to tout exercise as "nature's own tranquilizer." He and others believe that this tranquilizing effect occurs in part because endurance exercise triggers the release of endorphins, hormones produced by the pituitary gland in the brain. Once endorphins enter the bloodstream, their beneficial effects are thought to last several hours. Those effects include euphoria, a feeling that all is right with the world.[20]

Feeling less anxious about your condition is wonderful, of course. But feeling healthier and being able to conduct your affairs with more gusto and less disability is even better. This is what the medical community calls an *improved quality of life*. Researchers from the Cleveland Clinic report that an improved quality of life is precisely what 16 breathing disorder patients achieved in a 6-week rehabilitation program.[21]

PROVIDES FINANCIAL ADVANTAGES

The estimated health-care costs for treating COPD each year are staggering—some $26 billion in the United States alone. COPD ranks second only to heart disease in terms of the number of Americans (more than 500,000 to be exact) receiving Social Security disability payments for it.[5] And COPD is the reason for more than 5% of doctors' office visits annually and almost 13% of hospitalizations.[22]

Several studies on the monetary aspect of pulmonary exercise rehabilitation programs reveal that COPD patients who participate in such comprehensive programs spend much less time in the hospital and pay less for medical services than those who do not. In one study of 80 COPD patients, there was a 68% decrease in hospital days in the year following rehab compared to the year before rehab. This study continued to monitor the same patients for 8 years. The rehab graduates maintained their lower-hospital-days tally over the long term. The researchers calculated an average total savings of $416,000, or $5,200 per patient, per year.[23] The evidence indicates that, even in pure dollar terms, a comprehensive pulmonary rehabilitation program is a cost-effective investment.

By now I hope I've convinced you of the many benefits of a physically active lifestyle for persons with breathing disorders. But please keep in mind that exercise is not a panacea, but an important supplemental

Dollar advantages of exercise

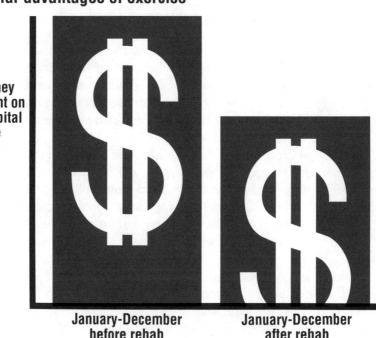

Money spent on hospital care

January-December before rehab

January-December after rehab

therapy. To be most effective, regular exercise must be combined with appropriate medical care and other positive lifestyle changes (stopping smoking and eating nutritiously, for example).

EXERCISE RISKS

There are some risks to exercise. The major health hazards for all *vigorous* exercisers, whether or not they have respiratory problems, are cardiac complications and musculoskeletal injuries. For you, a COPD patient, there's the additional risk that the wrong kind of exercise, or too much of it, can precipitate an asthma attack or cause *hypoxemia*, a dangerous dive in your blood-oxygen concentration.

Cardiac Complications

You've probably read or heard about people who drop dead suddenly from a heart attack while exercising. It's a chilling picture, to be sure—one that might make you wonder if it's really safe to exercise, especially if you're up in years.

Studies make it clear that it's not exercise itself that's dangerous. It's the lethal combination of injudicious, vigorous exertion and preexisting coronary artery disease, which you may not know you have. In chapter 5, I'll tell you how to determine whether you have coronary artery disease and, if you do, how to minimize your risk of experiencing a potentially fatal cardiac event during exercise. Following my guidelines is important because about 50% of COPD patients over 50 years old are known to have heart disease.[24]

In addition to coronary artery disease, one other heart disorder may be of concern to you: cor pulmonale, which, as I mentioned earlier in this chapter, predisposes a person to heart failure. Cor pulmonale shouldn't stop you from exercising, provided you're being adequately treated for it and you follow my safe-exercise guidelines.

If you are still skeptical, consider this: When appropriate precautions are taken, exercise is exceptionally safe even for people with heart disease or who've had heart attacks.[25] Amazing as it seems, many people who have undergone a lung transplant or a combined heart-lung transplant can exercise.[26,27] Generally, heart and lung ailments are a reason to exercise, not a reason to write it off.

Hypoxemia and Exercise-Induced Asthma

What about exertion for people prone to these conditions? For some COPD patients, it doesn't even take exertion to trigger hypoxemia, a condition in which the lungs are unable to provide the blood flowing through them with adequate oxygen, making the blood-oxygen concentration low. For others, exertion is the precursor. To be sure, hypoxemia should be avoided at all costs. Even a short bout of hypoxemia can harm the brain and heart, which are extremely sensitive to oxygen deprivation. And prolonged hypoxemia can cause cor pulmonale and can also substantially increase your risk of dying prematurely.[28,29]

As you'll learn in chapter 5, your doctor can easily determine if you're at risk for developing hypoxemia during exercise. If you are, you'll need to use supplemental oxygen when you work out. Exercise-induced asthma is also relatively easy to pinpoint and, in most cases, not difficult to prevent. I'll discuss both problems in chapter 5.

Musculoskeletal Injuries

Even adults with no health problems occasionally sustain musculoskeletal injuries during exercise. Two recent studies estimate that 50% of competitive runners sustain at least one exercise-related injury each year.[30,31] Keep in mind, these are serious amateur or professional runners. When the sample involves only recreational exercisers, the story is much different. Such studies, including one conducted at The Cooper Institute for Aerobics Research,[32] suggest that the number of exercise-induced injuries among noncompetitive athletes is not nearly as high as popularly believed. In fact, it's estimated that musculoskeletal injuries serious enough to require medical care probably occur at an annual rate of less than 5% among recreational exercisers. In chapter 5, I'll tell you how to minimize your risk for such injuries.

Chapter 2
Prescription

❏ Include exercise in your breathing disorder treatment and rehabilitation program.
❏ Exercise regularly to help relieve your breathlessness and to minimize your long-term disability.
❏ Exercise regularly to reduce your risk for premature death.

❏ Exercise regularly to improve your mental outlook and quality of life.

❏ Exercise regularly to enhance your productivity and reduce the economic burden of your breathing disorder.

❏ Keep in mind that exercise is not a panacea, but an important supplemental therapy.

❏ To gain optimal benefits, combine regular exercise with appropriate medical care and other positive lifestyle changes.

❏ Be aware that inappropriate exercise could worsen any complications that may have resulted from your breathing disorder.

❏ Obtain your doctor's consent before beginning an exercise program.

Chapter 3

Getting Started on a Regular Exercise Program

You might want to think of exercise as a form of breathing disorder medication. When you exercise, just as when you take drugs, you have twin goals: effectiveness and safety. You must strike a balance between the two.

This chapter and the next will focus on effectiveness. I'll explain which types of exercise, and how much of each, you need to do to derive maximum health benefits. In chapter 5 I'll discuss safety.

COMPONENTS OF AN EXERCISE WORKOUT

A typical exercise session should consist of 10 to 20 minutes of stretching and muscle-strengthening exercises; 5 minutes of aerobic warm-up; 15 to 60 minutes of aerobic exercise at an appropriate intensity; 5 minutes of aerobic cool-down; and, finally, 5 minutes of stretching. Note that stretching and muscle strengthening are included at the beginning, and stretching exercises are repeated at the end of the workout. It may take you several weeks to gradually work up to the durations I've specified.

What's the rationale for doing these various forms of exercise? The aerobic portion of the workout, of course, is aimed squarely at what is probably your most important goal: reducing the breathlessness you feel when you exert yourself. In the long term, it should also reduce your risk for other chronic ailments, particularly heart disease. Yes, the aerobic part is the most important. But don't overlook stretching and strengthening your muscles. After all, without well-functioning muscles, you can't undertake aerobics or many other recreational, occupational, and self-care activities. Also, without strong, flexible muscles, you're more likely to sustain a musculoskeletal injury. Indeed, the stretching and strengthening components of a balanced exercise program are so important that The Cooper Institute for Aerobics Research has published a book, *The Strength Connection*, that deals almost exclusively with them.[1]

Also, weak muscles are thought to be an important reason why the typical exercise performance of COPD patients is poor.[2] Weak thigh muscles contribute to premature fatigue during walking, stair climbing, and other activities that rely heavily on the legs. Weak upper body muscles may evoke excessive breathlessness during activities performed with the arms held in an unsupported position.[3,4] Examples of such activities are brushing your hair, hanging a picture on the wall, and stacking bookshelves. And studies show that muscle strengthening reduces a person's ventilatory requirements and thus lessens the tendency toward breathlessness during exercise.[5,6]

Stretching Exercises

Stretching is part of a good exercise protocol. It should always precede an aerobic exercise session, whether or not you have a breathing disorder. It won't take you long to appreciate the value of stretching. It relaxes you mentally and physically and probably helps prevent injuries by increasing your flexibility and widening your freedom of movement.

At the beginning of an exercise session, and if you have time at the end (and I encourage you to make time), do 1 to 3 repetitions of several of the stretches shown and described in Figures 3.1-3.5. Each stretch should be held for 10 to 20 seconds with no bouncing. Do not stretch to the point where the exercise becomes painful. Remember to keep breathing regularly—do not hold your breath.

Over the years, I have found these exercises to be particularly useful. However, if you have had previous joint surgery or have any musculoskeletal problems, such as arthritis, please check with your doctor before doing them.

Figure 3.1
Shoulder and Back Stretch.   Lift your right elbow toward the ceiling and place your right hand as far down your back between the shoulder blades as possible. Allow your chin to rest on your chest. If possible, using your left hand, gently pull your right elbow to the left until a stretch is felt on the back of the right arm and down the right side of the back. Hold. Repeat with the left arm.

Figure 3.2
Inner Thigh Stretch.   Sit on the floor, place the soles of your feet together, and pull your heels in as close to the buttocks as possible. Gently press your knees down toward the floor.

Figure 3.3
Lower Back and Hamstring Stretch.   Sitting on the floor with your legs straight out in front of you and your hands on your thighs, bend forward slowly, reaching toward your toes. Keep your head and back aligned as you move into the stretch. If necessary, you can bend your knees slightly.

Figure 3.4
Lower Back, Thigh, and Hip Stretch.   Lie flat on your back with your legs extended on the floor. Pull your right knee up to your chest and press your back to the floor. Hold this position and then repeat with the left knee.

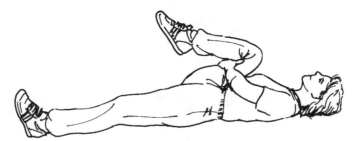

Figure 3.5
Calf Stretch.   Stand facing a wall, approximately 3 feet away. Place your palms on the wall, keeping your feet flat on the floor. Leave one foot in place as you step forward with the other. Make sure your back

remains straight as you gently bend the front knee forward toward the wall. Repeat the same exercise with the opposite leg.

Muscle-Strengthening Exercises

In contrast to flexibility training, which you should include in all your workouts, muscle-strengthening exercises need to be done only 2 or 3 days a week—and *not* on consecutive days. But even this minimal amount of strength training may be too much for some of you. Although it's safe for people with uncomplicated breathing disorders, muscle strengthening with heavy weights can cause an excessive rise in the pressure inside your chest as well as in your blood pressure. Because of this, it may be dangerous for anyone who is prone to an exercise-induced drop in their blood-oxygen concentration (hypoxemia) or who has cardiovascular disease. If you fall into either of these categories yet have received clearance from your doctor to proceed with muscle strengthening, pay special attention to the following words of caution:

• *Don't hold a contraction for more than about 6 seconds.* Isometric exercise—a static type of strength building in which a muscle remains contracted for more than a few seconds without relaxing—can elicit adverse cardiac responses in patients with cardiovascular disease.

• *Avoid holding your breath.* A Valsalva maneuver during lifting— that is, exhaling forcefully without releasing the air from the lungs—is also ill-advised because it predisposes you to hypoxemia, pushes up blood pressure, and places increased stress on your respiratory and cardiovascular systems. Exhale on the most strenuous part of an exercise.

- *Do not undertake activities where you must hold weight above your head for more than a few seconds.* Such movements cause a greater-than-expected increase in the ventilatory requirements of COPD patients and also place an excessive load on the cardiovascular systems of people with cardiovascular disease.

- *Substitute lighter weights (or less resistance) for heavier weights (or greater resistance) and do more repetitions.* Do not use the heavier weights with the idea that you'll just exercise for a shorter time. Heavier weights increase your blood pressure more than lighter ones.

I've developed an easy muscle-strengthening program you can do at home. It's based on the use of resistive rubber bands that are inexpensive (around $10), versatile, and convenient to use. Several types are available. Dyna-Bands and Therabands, two of the most popular, can be ordered from The Hygenic Corporation, 1245 Home Ave., Akron, OH 44310; phone 216-633-8460. Here's how you exercise with them:

You either pull or push against the bands, which resist your efforts. The amount of resistance varies according to the band thickness, and the bands are color-coded to indicate thickness. You can exercise with one band only or use them in combination for greater resistance.

Here are some more exercise safety tips to bear in mind:

- Before you begin to exercise, remove all jewelry, even a watch, from your arms.
- If you have arthritis in your hands or fingers, it may be a challenge to keep the band from slipping out of your grip. If so, you can tie loops at each end and attach them around your hands or wrists. Tying the loops will require ordering bands longer than the standard 36 inches.
- Some exercises require you to tie the band so it forms a loop. Use a knot or a half-bow, which is easier to undo.
- When wrapping a band around any body part, do it so you're still comfortable. It should never be too tight.
- Begin your exercise sequence with the thinnest band, which provides the least resistance. As tolerance permits, gradually progress to the thicker bands.
- During the exercise, always try to maintain the natural width of the band. Don't let it fold over.
- Exercise 3 days a week on alternate days.
- For each exercise, do 8 to 16 slow, complete, and controlled repetitions. Each execution should take from 3 to 5 seconds,

and your movements should be smooth and continuous. Never jerk your band or allow it to snap back. Always keep some tension on the band as it returns to its starting position; you can relax completely for 2 to 3 seconds between repetitions. You control the band—don't let it control you.

- Take from 15 to 60 seconds to rest between each set, longer if necessary. (The full number of repetitions ordered for each exercise is referred to as a *set*.) Once you can do two complete sets (2 × 16 repetitions for each exercise) with relative ease, you may want to progress to a thicker, more resistant band. But remember, it's more important to do the exercises correctly than to increase the resistance.
- Maintain good posture throughout the exercise sequence.
- Don't hold your breath during repetitions. If you feel inclined to do so, the band may afford too much resistance for your current strength level. This is forcing you to strain when you shouldn't have to.
- Start slowly and progress gradually. If you're weak to start with, it won't take much exercise to improve your strength. In fact, one study suggests that people with weak muscles can increase their strength dramatically just by performing these exercises working against gravity, without adding any resistance.[7] Don't exceed a rating of perceived exertion (RPE) or rating of perceived breathlessness (RPB) of 3 during your first 6 to 8 weeks of muscle strengthening and of 5 thereafter (see Table 3.1 later in this chapter).

Although this program was designed specifically for patients whose respiratory or cardiovascular problems are receiving adequate treatment, you should still check with your doctor before starting it. The program, which works all the major muscles, is depicted in Figures 3.6-3.16. (Incidentally, contrary to the description of a typical exercise session on page 27, it's fine if you do muscle strengthening after, rather than before, the aerobic portion of your workout.)

Figure 3.6
Side Shoulder Raise (outer portion of the shoulders). Place your foot on one end of the band and grip the other end with the hand on the opposite side of your body. Start with your arm extended at your side and the palm of your hand facing the side of your thigh. Keeping your elbow slightly bent, raise your arm out at your side to

shoulder level. Slowly lower your arm to the starting position. Repeat this motion with the same arm until you fulfill your repetition goal. Then switch to the other arm and leg and repeat.

Figure 3.7
Front Shoulder Raise (front portion of the shoulders).   This is a variation of Figure 3.6. Once again, place your foot on one end of the band, but this time grip the other end with the hand on the same side of your body. Begin with your arm extended at your side and the palm of your hand facing the side of your thigh. Keeping your elbow slightly bent, raise your arm out in front of your body to shoulder level. Slowly lower your arm to the starting position. Repeat this motion with the same arm until you fulfill your repetition goal. Then switch to the other arm and leg and repeat.

Figure 3.8
Chest Press (chest muscles and upper back).   Loop the band around your upper back and grip the ends in your hands. Bend both elbows to a 90° angle. Lift both elbows away from your sides until they're at armpit level and your arms are almost parallel to the floor. This is your starting position. Press your arms forward until they're almost completely straight. Slowly bend your elbows until your hands return to the starting position. Repeat.

Figure 3.9
Biceps Curl (muscles in the front of the upper arm).   Place your foot on one end of the band and grip the other end with the hand on the same side of your body. Start with your arm extended at your side and the palm of your hand facing forward. Keeping your elbow close to your side, bend it so that your fist curls upward to your shoulder. Slowly lower your arm to the starting position. Repeat this motion

with the same arm until you fulfill your repetition goal. Then switch to the other arm and leg and repeat.

Figure 3.10
Triceps Extension (muscles in the back of the upper arm).   Take one step forward and place your front foot on one end of the band. Grip the other end with the hand on the opposite side of your body. Bend your front knee slightly, lean forward, and rest the hand on the same side of the body, palm down, on your knee. Place the other hand—the one holding the band—against your hip, palm facing inward. Gradually straighten that arm out fully behind you. Then slowly bend your arm until your hand returns to the starting position at your hip. Repeat this motion with the same arm until you fulfill your repetition goal. Then switch to the opposite arm and leg and repeat.

Figure 3.11

Seated Rowing Exercise (upper back, shoulders, and neck). Sit on the floor with your back upright and your knees either bent or straight, whichever is more comfortable. Grab each end of the band with your hands and loop the band around your feet. Start with your arms extended in front of you, your hands slightly lower than shoulder level, and your palms facing the floor. Pull both ends of the band toward your armpits, while maintaining good posture. Slowly return your hands to the starting position and repeat.

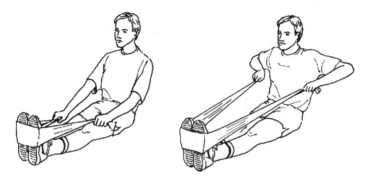

Figure 3.12

Seated Hip Abduction (hips and outer thighs). Sit on the floor with your back upright and your legs out straight in front of you. Place a knotted band around the outside of your ankles. Keep your legs straight as you brace yourself with palms on the floor just behind you. Slide your legs apart until you note significant resistance. Slowly return both legs to the starting position and repeat. To decrease the resistance, do this exercise with the band looped around the outside of your thighs just above the knees.

Figure 3.13
Half-Sit-Ups (abdominal muscles).   Lie on the floor with your knees bent at a 90° angle and the palms of your hands resting on the front of your thighs. Lift your shoulders off the floor and slide your fingers up toward your knees. Return to the horizontal starting position and repeat.

Figure 3.14
Calf Raises (calf muscles).   Stand with your fingers against a wall in front of you for balance. Rise up onto the balls of both feet. Lower your heels to the floor and repeat. Keep your knees straight throughout this exercise.

Figure 3.15

Standing Hip Flexion (hips and the front of the thighs).   Stand between the backrests of two chairs with your feet close together. Place a looped band around the outside of your ankles. Throughout this exercise, hold onto both backrests for balance and support and keep both knees slightly bent. Bracing yourself with your arms and keeping one foot in place, press the other leg forward until you encounter significant resistance. Slowly return your leg to the starting position and repeat with the opposite leg. For less resistance, do this exercise with the band looped around the outside of your thighs just above the knees.

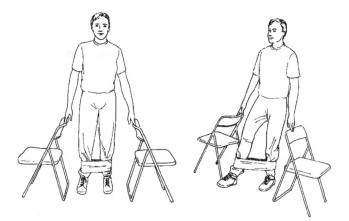

Figure 3.16

Standing Hip Extension (hips, back of the thighs, buttocks, and lower back muscles).   Stand between the backrests of two chairs with your feet close together. Place a looped band around the outside of your ankles. Throughout this exercise, hold onto both backrests for balance and support and keep both knees slightly bent. Bracing yourself with your arms and keeping one foot in place, press the other leg backward until you encounter significant resistance. Slowly return your leg to the starting position and repeat with the opposite leg. For less resistance, do this exercise with the band looped around the outside of your thighs just above the knees.

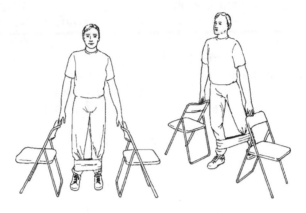

If your doctor clears you to undertake a more strenuous muscle-strengthening program, find a health professional who is familiar with your case to instruct you in the correct use of resistance-training equipment. A well-equipped gym might be outfitted with weight-training devices carrying such brand names as Cybex Strength Systems, Hydrafitness, Nautilus, and Universal. These are excellent machines, provided someone carefully instructs you on how to use them and supervises your exercise.

The American College of Sports Medicine recommends that the average healthy adult perform a minimum of 8 to 10 exercises using the major muscle groups at least twice weekly. The college further recommends that adults perform at least one set, consisting of 8 to 12 repetitions, of each exercise during each muscle-strengthening workout. These recommendations are appropriate for people with breathing disorders. But if you have heart disease, I suggest you consult *The Cooper Clinic Cardiac Rehabilitation Program*[8] for more extensive guidelines.

Aerobic Exercise

Ken Cooper actually coined the term *aerobics* in 1968 when his first book, *Aerobics*, was published.[9] Indeed, if you'd looked up the word *aerobic* in the dictionary before 1968, it would have been described as an adjective meaning "growing in air or in oxygen." It was commonly used to describe bacteria that need oxygen to live. Ken, however, coined the word *aerobics* as a noun to denote those forms of endurance exercises that require increased amounts of oxygen for prolonged periods of time. Proof of his influence came in the 1986 edition of the *Oxford English Dictionary*, in which aerobics is defined as "a method of physical exercise for producing beneficial changes in the respiratory and circulatory systems by activities which require only a modest increase of oxygen intake and so can be maintained."

The tricky issue is determining how much aerobic exercise is just enough to insure health benefits without increasing the chances that you'll injure yourself or have a medical emergency. Steven N. Blair, director of epidemiology at The Cooper Institute for Aerobics Research, and researchers from other medical institutions (including the Centers for Disease Control, Stanford University, and the University of Wisconsin) have examined this issue in depth.[10-12] They reviewed the findings of many exercise studies and identified an ideal upper and lower exercise limit. Future studies are needed, but there does appear to be a just-right level of exercise, which is actually a quite modest amount—far less than the strenuous workouts that exercise enthusiasts engage in as a matter of course. In the language of the exercise physiologist:

> Exercise training that results in a weekly energy expenditure of between *10 and 20 calories per kilogram of body weight** is likely to bring about major health benefits.[10,11] Twenty calories is the upper limit necessary from a health promotion standpoint— energy expenditures above this level do not appear to provide substantially more benefit.[10] The lower limit of 10 calories is necessary to insure effectiveness,[11] although lesser amounts are still likely to be of some benefit.[13]

Here are two examples: Dave Saxon weighed 165 pounds (75 kilograms) when he first arrived at The Cooper Aerobics Center. So Dave needed to gradually build up to an energy expenditure of between 750 (75 × 10) and 1,500 (75 × 20) calories during exercise each week. Another breathing disorder patient, Jenny Thompson, weighed 143 pounds (65 kilograms). Her target weekly energy expenditure during exercise was 650 (65 × 100) to 1,300 (65 × 20) calories.

These conclusions form the mathematical basis of the Health Points System described in the next chapter. Most patients would find it difficult to calculate how much exercise they need to do to expend 10 to 20 calories per kilogram of body weight. Our Health Points

---

*1 kilogram = approximately 2.2 pounds. 1 calorie = approximately 4.2 kilojoules.

System transforms these seemingly complicated recommendations into a practical, easy-to-follow method to assess the effectiveness of your exercise program. So if you're concerned about the complexity of calculating your weekly energy expenditure, stop worrying—our Health Points System will take care of this for you.

Factors That Determine Energy Expenditure

Weekly energy expenditure during exercise depends largely on four factors: the *type*, *frequency*, *intensity*, and *duration* of your exercise sessions. It's these four major considerations that you and your doctor should discuss in tailoring a safe and effective weekly exercise regimen for you. Keeping both your medical condition and personal preferences in mind, your doctor should help you

- choose a suitable aerobic exercise,
- decide on the number of times you should work out each week,
- determine the appropriate intensity at which to exercise, and
- establish how long each exercise session should last.

It's important for you to understand how the last three items intertwine. They're embodied in the concept of FIT, which is an acronym for **F**requency, **I**ntensity, and **T**ime. If you exercise regularly, you're undoubtedly familiar with this notion already. *Frequency* refers to how often you exercise. *Intensity* refers to how hard you exert yourself. *Time* refers to each exercise session's duration. An equation showing their interrelationship would look like this:

$$\text{Frequency} + \text{Intensity} + \text{Time} = \text{Caloric Energy Expenditure}$$
$$= \text{Health Benefit}$$

Clearly, if the amount on the right side of the equation (caloric energy expenditure and health benefit) remains constant and you cut down on one or two elements on the left side of the equation, the third element on the left side of the equation must increase to make up the difference. For example, if you exercise at a low to moderate intensity 3 days a week, each exercise session may have to last a relatively long time if you're to get enough exercise to substantially affect your health. Instead you may choose to exercise at the same low to moderate intensity but for a shorter length of time each session. In this instance, you'll have to increase the number of times per week that you exercise to achieve the desired weekly energy expenditure.

Here are my recommendations concerning each of these factors:

Frequency. I recommend that healthy people exercise 3 to 5 days per week. And my advice is the same for people with breathing disorders. Less is unlikely to produce significant health improvements; more predisposes you to musculoskeletal injuries. Space your workouts throughout the week. For example, if you're a 3-day-a-week exerciser, rather than training Monday, Tuesday, and Wednesday, you'd be better off training Monday, Wednesday, and Friday.

Time or Duration. The higher the intensity or frequency, the shorter the time needed to attain the desired weekly energy expenditure. Moderate-intensity aerobic exercise of longer duration is preferable to high-intensity exercise of shorter duration for these reasons: It lessens the risk of training-related complications, particularly cardiac complications and hypoxemia; it lessens your ventilatory requirement (the amount of air your lungs must breathe to meet your body's needs during exercise, which I discussed in chapter 2) and, thus, decreases the tendency toward breathlessness; and it is less stressful on your musculoskeletal system. Additionally, the average person is more likely to enjoy moderate workouts. Longer, moderate workouts are particularly important if you're trying to lose weight because they promote fat loss while reducing the risk of musculoskeletal injuries.

Workouts of 20 to 45 minutes of continuous aerobic exercise are what most of you should aim to gradually build up to. But because of your breathing disorder, you might want to consider a viable alternative that has been documented by researchers at Stanford University. They found that three 10-minute exercise sessions spread throughout the day may yield fitness gains similar to one 30-minute session.[14] This finding should be welcome news to all COPD patients who find that shorter exercise sessions result in less breathlessness. It's also good news for people with exercise-induced asthma. For reasons no one fully understands, an exercise bout that brings on an asthma attack "cures" a person from experiencing another one when he or she resumes exercising. This "curative" effect seems to last up to 4 hours after the first attack.[15]

These recommendations on duration do not include the warm-up and cool-down periods that should open and close each aerobics session. Take at least 5 minutes to ease into aerobics, starting at a low intensity and slowly building up to your peak, target intensity. Also, reduce your exercise intensity gradually for at least 5 minutes at the end of your workout.

Intensity. It's a fallacy to assume that you must exercise at high intensities to derive health benefits. In short, the "no pain, no gain" axiom is wrong. It's an especially dangerous idea for people who have an enlarged right side of their heart (cor pulmonale), exercise-induced hypoxemia, or other chronic ailments such as coronary artery disease. Optimal health benefits can be derived with minimum risk when a person exercises at moderate rather than high intensity.

How to Quantify Exercise Intensity

There are a number of ways to quantify exercise intensity, and I'll discuss three. You can quantify it in terms of metabolic equivalent units (METs), heart rate, or perceived exertion and breathlessness.

METs. One MET is the amount of oxygen your body consumes for energy production each minute while you're at rest. If you're engaged in an activity corresponding to 5 METs, your body is taking up and using five times more oxygen than it did at rest. This is the amount it now needs to fuel your working muscles, enabling them to produce the required amount of energy. I'll return to the subject of METs later in this chapter when I explain how to select an appropriate speed or work rate for the initial weeks of a walking or stationary cycling exercise program.

Heart Rate. This is perhaps the most widely used and helpful way to target exercise intensity. This method is based on the principle that there's a direct relationship between the increase in your body's oxygen uptake during exertion and the increase in your heart rate.

I advise my patients with breathing disorders to exercise at an intensity that raises the heart rate above 60% of their maximal heart rate but no higher than 85%. That's an exercise training zone range spanning 25 percentage points.

What's your *maximal heart rate*? It's the highest heart rate that you can attain during exercise without becoming so fatigued or out of breath that you have to stop—or without developing significant cardiovascular or respiratory abnormalities. Maximal heart rate can differ considerably from one person to the next.

The most accurate way to determine your maximal heart rate is to have a treadmill or cycle test. In medical jargon, this is called a *symptom-limited maximal exercise test*; the term *symptom-limited* simply means that you exercise until you cannot continue, either because you are too fatigued or out of breath or because you develop an excessive drop in blood-oxygen concentration or certain ECG or other abnormalities that indicate to your physician that the test should be stopped. The American College of Sports Medicine recommends an exercise test for all patients with breathing disorders. I go along with the ACSM's position and strongly advocate this test for all our patients with breathing disorders.[16] I urge you to have an exercise test, if at all possible. Among other things, the test will enable your doctor to tell you the highest heart rate you're able to achieve without developing any potentially dangerous pulmonary or cardiovascular problems. *This is the value you should use as your maximal heart rate.*

Both Dave Saxon and another client, Jenny Thompson, had exercise tests. Dave's maximal heart rate was 150 beats per minute. Jenny's was 184 beats per minute. If you don't have a test, you can *estimate* your maximal heart rate using the following formula:

For all women and sedentary men:	
220 minus your age in years	= Estimated Maximal Heart Rate
For conditioned men:	
205 minus one-half your age in years	= Estimated Maximal Heart Rate

For example, Dave at age 66 had an estimated maximal heart rate of 154 beats per minute (220 − 66 = 154). At age 43, Jenny's estimated maximal heart rate was 177 beats per minute (220 − 43 = 177) before she began our supervised exercise program. Note that Dave's actual maximal heart rate was 150, slightly lower than his estimate. Jenny's (184) was slightly higher.

Be aware that these formulas are not valid for people taking medications that slow down the heart rate. For safety reasons, I also caution people who know they have heart disease to ignore these formulas, whether they're taking medication or not.

Training Target Heart Rate Zone.   Once you know your maximal heart rate (either estimated using the formula or based on an exercise test), it's easy to determine the limits you should stay within when you exercise. As I mentioned previously, I recommend that you push your heart rate above 60% of your maximal heart rate but no higher than 85%. This is your *training target heart rate zone*, which you calculate by multiplying your maximal heart rate by the lower limit of 60% (or 0.6) and the upper limit of 85% (or 0.85).

Using Dave's actual maximal heart rate of 150, he calculated a lower limit of 90 beats per minute (150 × 0.6 = 90) and an upper limit of 128 beats per minute (150 × 0.85 = 128). Jenny's training heart rate zone was between 110 (184 × 0.6 = 110) and 156 (184 × 0.85 = 156) beats per minute.

This zone is important. Studies show that exercise performed at an intensity lower than 60% may net you some health benefits but is unlikely to substantially increase your fitness level. And if you don't exceed the 60% mark, you'll probably have to lengthen each exercise session to well over an hour to attain the recommended weekly energy expenditure.

Some COPD patients are too unfit or disabled by their breathing disorder to tolerate exercise above the 60% lower limit, especially if their training target heart rate zone was estimated using the formula rather than measured during an exercise test. These patients often must exercise at lower heart rates until their exercise tolerance improves to where they can exercise at higher intensities.[17] During this time they should work on gradually increasing the duration of their exercise sessions. Another possibility is *interval training*[16]—doing a series of bouts of exercise, each separated by a short rest period, rather than one long, endurance-oriented workout.

Here's how interval training might work: Instead of cycling without stopping for 30 minutes at the desired heart rate, you'd divide the session into six mini-sessions. You'd alternate cycling for 5 minutes with cycling at a very low intensity or resting completely for 1 minute to reduce temporarily any breathlessness or fatigue. (Incidentally, low-intensity cycling is preferable to a complete stop because abrupt cessation of exertion may cause a dangerous drop in your blood pressure.)

It's especially crucial that those of you with any cardiovascular problems never exceed the 85% upper limit. High-intensity exercise increases the risk for triggering cardiac complications during exercise. Even if you're not aware of such problems, I still encourage people with a breathing disorder to stay below the 85% ceiling. The only exceptions are competitive athletes and, under certain circumstances, COPD patients who exercise under medical supervision.[18,19]

Using Heart Rate to Guide Intensity. For novice exercisers, the questions and answers that follow will give you more insight into how to use your heart rate as a guide to exercise intensity.

- *How do I measure my heart rate during exercise?* The same way you'd do it at rest, by taking your pulse. (See Appendix A.)

• *How often during exercise should I calculate my heart rate?* Initially, you may need to check your heart rate as often as every 5 minutes. Once you are familiar with your appropriate exercise intensity, though, you may need to do it only a few times each workout. I generally recommend that you check your rate at the following times:

1. *Before starting to exercise.* If it is above 100 beats per minute and remains this high after 15 minutes or so of rest, don't exercise at all. This is probably caused by bronchodilator medication you may be taking for your breathing problem, but it's best to check this out with your doctor.

2. *After you complete your warm-up.* If your heart rate is above your upper limit (85%) at this point, slow down until it drops below this limit. You performed your warm-up at too high an intensity. Start off slower next time.

3. *After you've been exercising at your peak intensity for about 5 minutes.* If it is above your upper limit, slow down and recheck it within 5 minutes.

4. *When you stop the aerobic phase and begin your cool-down.*

5. *When you complete your cool-down.* If your heart rate isn't below 100 beats per minute, rest until it reaches this level. Only then should you take a shower or drive off in your car.

• *Can I rely on a portable heart rate monitor instead of checking my heart rate manually?* Commercially available meters are generally worn on the chest and provide continuous monitoring of your heart rate by transmitting electrical signals to a special wristwatch or computer that's also worn on your chest. Usually, you can program your heart rate limit into the device, which will set off an alarm if you exceed your limit. Provided you purchase a reliable model, such monitors can be helpful, but they're certainly not a necessity.

Consult a member of your health-care team before buying one. Ask which type he or she thinks is most accurate. Then before you purchase a specific one, ask that team member to help you verify its accuracy while you're wearing it.

Perceived Exertion or Breathlessness.   One of the simplest ways to quantify your exercise intensity is to use either of the two scales I've reproduced in Table 3.1. They're named after the Swedish exercise physiologist, Gunnar Borg, who originated the scale from which they're derived. The Borg scales help you judge your exercise intensity based on your on-the-spot perception of how hard the exercise feels or how out of breath you are.[20] The *rating of perceived exertion*

(RPE) and *rating of perceived breathlessness* (RPB) are outlined in Table 3.1. Both use scales running from 0 to 10 that you consult as you exercise. If you're exerting yourself at a level that you feel is fairly strenuous or causes what you consider to be moderate breathlessness, you might assign yourself a rating of 3. When you reach all-out huffing-and-puffing, you'd choose a much higher rating of about 7.

You should not force yourself to endure extreme discomfort during exercise because, in addition to being unpleasant, it could be dangerous.[21] I suggest that you aim for an RPE or RPB rating of 3 or 4 during the aerobic portion of your workout,[5] which is what our breathing disorders patients generally feel comfortable with. Unless you're exercising with a health-care professional standing by, you're a competitive athlete, or your doctor has given the OK, *never exceed a score of 5*—even if your heart rate is below your prescribed limit.

Table 3.1
Borg Scales

Use only one of these scales as a monitoring device during exercise. If fatigue is what tends to limit you during aerobic workouts, use the exertion scale on the left. If getting out of breath quickly is more of a problem, use the right-hand scale. As you can see, the scales are similar. If there's any doubt in your mind about which to use, I recommend the exertion scale. It's the one that's widely used throughout the world.

Rating of perceived exertion or RPE		Rating of perceived breathlessness or RPB	
0	Nothing at all	0	Nothing at all
0.5	Very, very weak	0.5	Very, very slight
1	Very weak	1	Very slight
2	Weak	2	Slight
3	Moderate	3	Moderate
4	Somewhat strong	4	Somewhat severe
5	Strong	5	Severe
6		6	
7	Very strong	7	Very severe
8		8	
9	Very, very strong	9	Very, very severe
10	Maximal	10	Maximal

Note. From G.A. Borg, "Psychophysical Bases of Perceived Exertion," *Medicine and Science in Sports and Exercise, 14*, pp. 377-387, 1982. Also, R.C. Wilson & P.W. Jones, "A Comparison of the Visual Analogue Scale and Modified Borg Scale for the Measurement of Dyspnoea During Exercise," *Clinical Science, 76*, pp. 277-282, 1989.

Basic Aerobic Exercises to Get You Started

Aerobic exercises *don't* require excessive speed or strength, but they *do* place demands on your cardiovascular and respiratory systems. In contrast, *anaerobic* exercise, as the prefix implies, means without oxygen. Sprinting is an anaerobic activity. It involves an all-out burst of effort and relies on metabolic processes that do not require oxygen for energy production. Such processes cause fatigue quickly.

Of the two, aerobic exercise is far better for people with breathing disorders who want to improve their health and fitness for these reasons: Energy expenditure is related to how much oxygen your working muscles use during exercise. Aerobic exercise uses up more oxygen than anaerobic exercise. Also, because it's more moderate and you can do it longer, aerobic exercise allows you to expend more energy than anaerobic exercise. Furthermore, when you exercise aerobically, you can better monitor your heart rate and keep it within your prescribed limits. And because anaerobic exercise causes the active muscles to produce large amounts of lactic acid, it greatly increases your ventilatory requirements and, thus, is likely to result in severe breathlessness.

The aerobic exercises I most commonly recommend for breathing disorder patients beginning an exercise program are walking, cycling, and, for those with Grade 1 breathlessness (see chapter 2), jogging. Each has its pluses and minuses.

Walking. Walking is one of the most appropriate aerobic activities for adults with breathing problems.[22] It's simple and straightforward, requiring no special skill, setting, or equipment other than a good pair of shoes. Walking is also one of the exercises least likely to cause or aggravate musculoskeletal problems. The intensity is easy to control, so many COPD patients with respiratory complications and other chronic diseases can walk and get the desired conditioning effect. And the findings of a recent study, conducted by Tom R. Thomas and Ben R. Londeree, suggest that the energy expenditure for walking at fast speeds approaches that for jogging.[23]

Perhaps the most important benefit to be gained from walking relates to the specificity of exercise training. This exercise physiology concept means that becoming fit by doing one form of aerobic exercise does not necessarily make you equally fit for another. In other words, if you train by walking rather than cycling, your ability to walk without becoming excessively fatigued or breathless will increase to a far greater degree than your ability to cycle without fatigue, and vice versa.

Why is this? First, many physiological adaptations that occur with exercise training take place in the muscles used during a specific exercise. Second, when you do a set of motions over and over (walking, for example), you become biomechanically more efficient in performing them. You walk with better posture, improved stride, and with fewer unnecessary movements.[24] This reduces your ventilatory requirement for a given amount of exercise.

The single most important cause of disability in COPD patients is severe breathlessness while walking. Clearly, improving your ability to walk without breathlessness is a key to feeling better, becoming more productive, and being able to fend for yourself.

Jogging. The advantages of jogging are similar to those for walking. The catch is that during jogging your feet strike the ground with a force that's about three to four times your body weight. This force is transmitted to your weight-bearing joints and, over time and done to excess, could lead to musculoskeletal injuries. (In contrast to jogging, walking exerts a force of one to one-and-a-half times your weight on the weight-bearing joints.[25]) Jogging also usually requires greater exertion, or intensity, than walking, often inducing breathlessness or a heart rate higher than your limit. And jogging is one of the physical activities most likely to precipitate exercise-induced asthma in susceptible people.[26] But if you decide to jog, despite the greater risks, I recommend you start with a walking program, then a walk-jog regimen. When they approach it sensibly, many patients with milder breathing problems can eventually include jogging in their training program with success.

Stationary Cycling. This is an activity busy people love. While you pedal away on your stationary cycle (also known as a *cycle ergometer*), you can do other things, like read or watch TV. Stationary cycling gives you no excuse should the weather make outdoor cycling impossible, and it causes less wear and tear on the musculoskeletal system than many aerobic activities, including even walking. To reduce the stress on your knees, set the saddle height so that your knee joints straighten almost fully during pedaling.

Cycling has a disadvantage, though. During a long ride, you may develop sore buttocks. To avoid this, our patients often combine stationary cycling with walking.

Some stationary cycles, such as the Schwinn Air-Dyne, allow you to achieve higher energy expenditures by working your arms and legs simultaneously. You pump your legs up and down while you move your arms forward and back. The result is a more thorough upper and lower body workout with less stress on your lower limb joints. I recommend these cycle ergometers for many breathing disorder patients, especially those who use their arms a lot at work or for recreation. I do so because, according to the specificity of exercise training principle, exercise that works your upper body muscles will help reduce fatigue and breathlessness during activities in which you use your arm muscles.

Arm-Cycle Ergometry. This is one alternative for patients who have lower limb problems such as arthritis, paraplegia, and peripheral vascular disease—problems that prevent them from using their legs during exercise—but whose arms are relatively unaffected. But because the upper limb muscles are smaller than the lower limb muscles, arm-cycle ergometry requires you to work harder to achieve a given energy expenditure. Also, for a given energy expenditure, the ventilatory requirement (and, hence, the degree of breathlessness) is greater with arm exercise than for leg exercise or combined arm/leg exercise. This is why the American College of Sports Medicine does not consider predominantly upper body aerobic exercises such as arm-cycle ergometry suitable for people with breathing disorders.[16]

Outdoor Cycling. In my opinion, outdoor cycling is far more enjoyable and exhilarating than pedaling away indoors. The disadvantage over a stationary workout is that roads tend to go up and down. An unexpected incline could cause an excessive rise in your ventilatory requirements or in your heart rate. Also, too many downhill stretches and excessive delays at traffic lights may lessen your energy expenditure considerably and force you to work out longer to achieve the desired energy expenditure. And traffic can be dangerous. Still, if you can deal with these drawbacks, outdoor cycling is great.

PUTTING ON THOSE WALKING SHOES AND VENTURING FORTH

Here I offer you guidelines for beginning a walking, walk-jog, or stationary cycling exercise program. I recommend these forms of exercise to sedentary adult patients with breathing disorders because they're a good way to slowly ease into the routine of regular exercise. After you've completed an introductory 10 to 12 weeks or so following one of these programs, you'll be ready to start trying to earn the 50 to 100 weekly health points discussed in the next chapter.

Please note that these programs are intended as a guideline. Your individual circumstances may require you to progress more slowly than I have suggested.

Beginning Walking Program

Walking is a wonderful way for people with breathing disorders to get moving down the road to optimal health. But before you begin, you should ideally know your maximal MET value in order to estimate the speed (in mph or kph) at which you should walk during your first 12 weeks of exercise. Maximal MET value varies among individuals and depends on fitness level and severity of breathing problem. If you've undergone an exercise test—which I urge all breathing disorder patients to do—your doctor can provide you with your maximal MET value. If not, err on the side of caution and start at a comfortable speed that does not exceed what's recommended for a person with a maximal MET value of 5. Whether you know your maximal MET value or not, I strongly advise against exceeding 85% of your maximal heart rate and an RPE or RPB of 5 during these initial weeks. Table 3.2 on page 56 shows you what your estimated beginning walking speed should be. (At fast speeds, the energy you expend for walking approaches that for jogging. Therefore, for speeds of 4 mph [or 6.4 kph] or faster, I recommend that you use the jogging chart in chapter 4 to calculate your health points.) Using Table 3.2, Dave Saxon, whose maximal MET value was 5, started his walking program at a speed of about 2.6 mph, or 4.2 kph. The box on page 56 shows you what your walking program will look like in terms of each workout's duration and frequency.

A Follow-Up Walk-Jog Program

Don't try jogging until you've followed a walking regimen for at least 6 weeks, ideally 12 weeks. In your walking program, you should be walking at speeds in excess of 4 mph just before you graduate to jogging. If you're walking at a slower rate, you might as well stay with walking. Here are some pointers:

- When you start to jog, do so at a speed no faster than that at which you currently walk.
- As always, warm up and cool down for at least 5 minutes each. For the warm-up phase, walk briskly and try to gradually raise

your heart rate to within at least 20 beats per minute of your target heart rate. On completing your jog, gradually reduce your speed to a slow walk over at least a 5-minute period. The box on pages 57-58 shows duration and frequency recommendations for your walk-jog program.

Beginning Stationary Cycling Program

If indoor cycling is more to your liking than walking, that's fine. It's an excellent form of exercise. Before you begin, you should ideally know your maximal MET value and your weight in either pounds or kilograms (in the boxes that follow, choose the weight closest to yours). If you haven't had an exercise test and don't know your maximal MET value, start at a comfortable work rate that does not exceed that recommended for a person with a maximal MET value of 5. Whether you know your maximal MET value or not, I strongly advise against exceeding 85% of your maximal heart rate and an RPE or RPB of 5 during these initial weeks. Table 3.3 on page 59 shows your estimated beginning work rate for a stationary cycling program. Jenny Thompson, who weighed 143 pounds and had a maximal MET value of 6, began her cycling program at 46 watts. Duration and frequency recommendations for the first 10 weeks of your cycling program are shown in the box on page 59.

Beginning Schwinn Air-Dyne Cycling Program

The Schwinn Air-Dyne, a second form of indoor cycling, which works both your arms and legs, is another good choice. Table 3.4 on page 60 shows how to estimate your work load for the first 10 weeks. If you don't know your maximal MET value, start at a comfortable work load of no more than that corresponding to a MET value of 5. Whether you know your maximal MET value or not, I strongly advise against exceeding 85% of your maximal heart rate and an RPE or RPB of 5 during these initial weeks. If you weigh 154 pounds (70 kilograms) and have a maximal MET value of 6, you would see by looking at Table 3.4 that you should cycle at a work load of 1.1.

The box on page 60 shows duration and frequency recommendations for your Schwinn Air-Dyne routine. A variety of other superb cycle ergometers also enable you to work your arms and legs simultaneously. If you prefer to use one of them, these recommendations are equally applicable.

Beginning Program of Combined Walking and Stationary Cycling Using the Schwinn Air-Dyne

Some people get bored doing the same exercise day after day. For such people, I've devised a 9-week regimen that combines walking with cycling on the Schwinn Air-Dyne. This combination will also help reduce your risk of injury.

The guidelines mentioned previously for walking and Schwinn Air-Dyne workouts apply. Use Tables 3.2 and 3.4 to estimate your starting walking speed and Schwinn Air-Dyne work load for the first 9 weeks of this program. Start with either activity. As always, warm up for at least 5 minutes. After completing the first activity, proceed immediately to the other one—another warm-up is not needed. Upon completing the second activity, cool down for at least 5 minutes. The duration and frequency recommendations are shown in the box on page 61.

THAT ALL-IMPORTANT TRAINING LOG

I encourage our breathing disorder patients to keep track of their exercise efforts, at least in the beginning, via a training log. A diary is a good idea because it provides you and your doctor with helpful data. And it will help you be consistent and stay on track with your exercise program. An empty training log page follows. I suggest that you make a number of photocopies of it and put them in a loose-leaf notebook. Fill in a page after each day's exercise.

DAILY EXERCISE TRAINING LOG

Date _____ Time of day _____ Body weight _____

Where I worked out _____

Weather conditions _____

Resting pulse _____

Resting blood pressure (if measured) _____

Inhaler used prior to exercise? Yes _____ No _____

Duration of stretching and strengthening portion
  of my workout _____

Pulse rate after stretching and strengthening portion
  of my workout (in beats per minute) _____

Aerobic portion of workout

  Type of exercise _____

  Duration (in minutes) _____

  Distance covered or work rate/load _____

  Highest heart rate during workout_____

  Borg RPE or RPB (at most intense part of workout) _____

  Any symptoms I experienced _____

  Inhaler used during exercise? Yes _____ No _____

  Supplemental oxygen used during exercise? Yes _ No _

Enjoyment rating _____ 1 Very unenjoyable

                 _____ 2 Unenjoyable

                 _____ 3 Somewhat unenjoyable

                 _____ 4 Enjoyable

                 _____ 5 Very enjoyable

Health points earned (see chapter 4) _____

Table 3.2
Estimated Speed at Which to Begin a Walking Program

Maximal MET value	Estimated walking speed (miles per hour)	Estimated walking speed (kilometers per hour)
3	1.0 mph	1.6 kph
4	1.8 mph	2.9 kph
5	2.6 mph	4.2 kph
6	3.4 mph	5.4 kph
7 and above	4.0 mph	6.4 kph

Walking Program		
Week	**Duration per session**	**Frequency per week**
1	2.5 minutes	3-5 times
2	5 minutes	3-5 times
3	7.5 minutes	3-5 times
4	10 minutes	3-5 times
5	12.5 minutes	3-5 times
6	15 minutes	3-5 times
7	20 minutes	3-5 times
8	25 minutes	3-5 times
9	30 minutes	3-5 times
10	35 minutes	3-5 times
11	40 minutes	3-5 times
12	45 minutes	3-5 times

13 and onward   It's time to start earning those 50 to 100 health points a week. Keep your exercise time at 45 minutes per session and gradually increase your speed until you exceed 60% of your maximal heart rate (if you are not doing so yet). If this does not result in the desired weekly energy expenditure using the health points charts in chapter 4,* do one or more of the following: Try exercising within the upper range of your target heart rate zone; exercise more frequently; or increase the duration of each exercise session.

Walk-Jog Program		
Week	**Duration per session**	**Frequency per week**
1	*20 minutes total*—Walk 4.5 min, jog 0.5 min, walk 4.5 min, jog 0.5 min, walk 4.5 min, jog 0.5 min, walk 4.5 min, jog 0.5 min*	3-5 times
2	*20 minutes total*—Walk 4 min, jog 1 min, walk 4 min, jog 1 min, walk 4 min, jog 1 min, walk 4 min, jog 1 min*	3-5 times
3	*20 minutes total*—Walk 3 min, jog 2 min, walk 3 min, jog 2 min, walk 3 min, jog 2 min, walk 3 min, jog 2 min*	3-5 times
4	*20 minutes total*—Walk 2 min, jog 3 min, walk 2 min, jog 3 min, walk 2 min, jog 3 min, walk 2 min, jog 3 min*	3-5 times
5	*20 minutes total*—Walk 5 min, jog 5 min, walk 5 min, jog 5 min*	3-5 times
6	*20 minutes total*—Walk 4 min, jog 6 min, walk 4 min, jog 6 min*	3-5 times
7	*20 minutes total*—Walk 3 min, jog 7 min, walk 3 min, jog 7 min*	3-5 times

(Cont.)

Walk-Jog Program (Continued)		
Week	**Duration per session**	**Frequency per week**
8	*20 minutes total* Jog 10 min, walk 10 min*	3-5 times
9	*20 minutes total*—Jog 12 min, walk 8 min*	3-5 times
10	*20 minutes total*—Jog 15 min, walk 5 min*	3-5 times
11	*20 minutes total*—Jog 17 min, walk 3 min*	3-5 times
12	*20 minutes total*—Jog 20 min*	3-5 times

13 and onward   By the time you reach this point, you are likely to have exceeded 60% of your maximal heart rate; and you've possibly attained your desired weekly energy expenditure—50 to 100 health points per week—using the health points charts in chapter 4.* If so, just keep following week 12's regimen. If, on the other hand, you haven't been able to exceed 60% of your maximal heart rate, increase your speed. If that does not result in 50 to 100 weekly health points, do one or more of the following: Try exercising within the upper range of your target heart rate zone; exercise more frequently; or increase the duration of each exercise session.

---

*You may find that you are below your desired weekly energy expenditure during the early weeks of this walk-jog effort. You can compensate by walking longer at the end of the jogging phase, before starting your cool-down. Use the jogging chart in chapter 4 when calculating your health points for your walk-jog program.

Table 3.3
Estimated Work Rate at Which to Begin
a Stationary Cycling (Legs Only) Program

	Work rate (watts)					
Maximal MET value	Body weight = 110 lb (50 kg)	Body weight = 132 lb (60 kg)	Body weight = 154 lb (70 kg)	Body weight = 176 lb (80 kg)	Body weight = 198 lb (90 kg)	Body weight = 220 lb (100 kg)
3	12	14	16	19	21	23
4	20	25	29	33	37	41
5	29	35	41	47	53	58
6	38	46	53	61	68	76
7	47	56	65	75	84	93
8 and above	55	67	78	89	100	111

Stationary Cycling Program

Week	Duration per session	Frequency per week
1	2.5 minutes	3-5 times
2	5 minutes	3-5 times
3	7.5 minutes	3-5 times
4	10 minutes	3-5 times
5	12.5 minutes	3-5 times
6	15 minutes	3-5 times
7	17.5 minutes	3-5 times
8	20 minutes	3-5 times
9	25 minutes	3-5 times
10	30 minutes	3-5 times

11 and onward   It's time to start earning those 50 to 100 health points a week. Keep your exercise time at 30 minutes per session and gradually increase your work rate until you exceed 60% of your maximal heart rate (if you are not doing so yet). If this does not result in the desired weekly energy expenditure using the health points charts in chapter 4, do one or more of the following: Try exercising within the upper range of your target heart rate zone; exercise more frequently; or increase the duration of each exercise session.

Table 3.4

**Estimated Work Load at Which to Begin
a Schwinn Air-Dyne Cycling Program**

	Work load					
Maximal MET value	Body weight = 110 lb (50 kg)	Body weight = 132 lb (60 kg)	Body weight = 154 lb (70 kg)	Body weight = 176 lb (80 kg)	Body weight = 198 lb (90 kg)	Body weight = 220 lb (100 kg)
3	.2	.3	.4	.4	.4	.5
4	.4	.5	.6	.7	.7	.8
5	.6	.7	.8	.9	1.1	1.2
6	.8	.9	1.1	1.2	1.4	1.5
7	.9	1.1	1.3	1.5	1.7	1.9
8 and above	1.1	1.3	1.6	1.8	2.0	2.2

Schwinn Air-Dyne Program

Week	Duration per session	Frequency per week
1	2.5 minutes	3-5 times
2	5 minutes	3-5 times
3	7.5 minutes	3-5 times
4	10 minutes	3-5 times
5	12.5 minutes	3-5 times
6	15 minutes	3-5 times
7	17.5 minutes	3-5 times
8	20 minutes	3-5 times
9	25 minutes	3-5 times
10	30 minutes	3-5 times

11 and onward   It's time to start earning those 50 to 100 health points a week. Keep your exercise time at 30 minutes per session and gradually increase your work load until you exceed 60% of your maximal heart rate (if you are not doing so yet). If this does not result in the desired weekly energy expenditure using the health points charts in chapter 4, do one or more of the following: Try exercising within the upper range of your target heart rate zone; exercise more frequently; or increase the duration of each exercise session.

Combined Walking and Schwinn Air-Dyne Program

	Duration per session		
Week	Walking	Schwinn Air-Dyne	Frequency per week
1	2.5 minutes	2.5 minutes	3-5 times
2	5 minutes	5 minutes	3-5 times
3	7.5 minutes	7.5 minutes	3-5 times
4	10 minutes	10 minutes	3-5 times
5	12.5 minutes	12.5 minutes	3-5 times
6	15 minutes	15 minutes	3-5 times
7	17.5 minutes	17.5 minutes	3-5 times
8	20 minutes	20 minutes	3-5 times
9	22.5 minutes	22.5 minutes	3-5 times

10 and onward   It's time to start earning those 50 to 100 health points a week. Keep the combined exercise time at 45 minutes per session and gradually increase the intensity until you exceed 60% of your maximal heart rate (if you're not doing so yet). If this does not result in the desired weekly energy expenditure using the health points charts in chapter 4, do one or more of the following: Try exercising within the upper range of your target heart rate zone; exercise more frequently; or increase the duration of each exercise session.

Chapter 3
Prescription

❏ Start your exercise program slowly and progress gradually as your condition permits.

❏ Always include a warm-up and cool-down—each lasting at least 5 minutes—in your exercise sessions.

❏ Do stretching and, unless contraindicated, aerobic exercise three to five times each week.

❏ Include muscle strengthening in your exercise routines two to three times each week.

❏ Structure the aerobic portion of your workout so that it is eventually 15 to 60 minutes long.

❏ Aim for an exercise intensity that raises your heart rate to between 60% and 85% of your maximal value and elicits an RPE or RPB of 3 to 4 during the aerobic portion of your workout.

❏ Don't exceed 85% of your maximal heart rate or an RPE or RPB of 5 at any point in your workout.

❏ Use interval training to lessen your breathlessness during exercise, if necessary.

❏ Exercise your options: Choose aerobic exercises that are convenient to perform.

❏ Keep track of your exercise efforts via a training diary.

Chapter 4

The Health Points System: Insuring Maximum Health Benefits With Minimum Risk

When I try to motivate patients with breathing problems to follow my exercise prescription, I have to juggle several responsibilities. First, as a physician, I must educate patients adequately so their excuse can never be "I didn't understand." Then I have to alert them to the seriousness of their condition, when appropriate, and the risks involved in exercise—without leaving them with the feeling it's hopeless. And, most importantly, I have to make them understand that drugs and medical care can only go so far in making them well. They must do the rest by making positive lifestyle changes, including following a regular exercise program.

The impetus for the Health Points System grew out of these various needs, especially the need to make you, the patient, responsible for your own health. The Health Points System gives you a way to chart how effective your exercise program is likely to be in promoting your health.* The system was devised so that patients would do just enough exercise to gain optimal health benefits without exerting themselves so much that exercise would be risky. As a person with a breathing disorder, you must strike a fine balance between effectiveness and safety. Our system incorporates both.

HOW THE HEALTH POINTS SYSTEM WORKS

Our system is based on the number of calories people of various weights expend during exercise. In chapter 3, I discussed what doctors and exercise physiologists have learned about aerobic exercise and its effect on health. Let's review a key finding:

> Aerobic exercise performed for 15 to 60 minutes per workout 3 to 5 days each week at an intensity that raises the heart rate to between 60% and 85% of the maximal value is likely to result in an energy expenditure that brings about the desired health benefits.

Here's how our Health Points System works. If you're a novice exerciser, consider following one of the beginning exercise programs outlined in chapter 3. Work up to an appropriate level of exertion gradually over 10 to 12 weeks or so. Although you can start using the Weekly Health Points Exercise Tally Sheet (see page 65) during this time, do not specifically try to earn 50 to 100 health points until you reach Weeks 10 to 12. Depending on the severity of your breathing disorder, it may take you longer than this—even months—to earn the desired number of points. That's fine. Be patient.

In all aspects of life, we humans like to know where we stand in our endeavors. We like to get report cards. The Health Points System is a kind of report card on your exercise program. Only you fill it out, not a doctor or a teacher. Our system enables you to quantify one constructive lifestyle change—namely, regular aerobic exercise—you can easily undertake. Regular aerobic exercise can improve your fitness, reduce your breathlessness during exertion, and lower your risk for heart disease and other serious chronic ailments. The Health Points

---

*Those of you with episodic asthma or COPD accompanied by mild breathlessness (Grade 1) and no other serious chronic diseases have the option of following Ken Cooper's well-known Aerobic Point System instead of our Health Points System. (He describes it fully in *The Aerobics Program for Total Well-Being.*[1])

WEEKLY HEALTH POINTS EXERCISE TALLY SHEET

Your Weekly Goal: To earn between 50 and 100 health points each week, which corresponds to an expenditure of 10 to 20 calories per kilogram (2.2 pounds) of body weight per week. Exceeding this upper limit does not provide substantially more health benefit; thus you should keep your weekly health points total at, or very near, 100. To gain optimal benefit, you should earn your weekly quota of points across at least 3 workouts.

To find out how many health points you earned during an exercise session, simply use the chart (see Tables 4.1-4.5, pages 77-84) that corresponds to the form of aerobic exercise you're doing and fill in the results below:

Monday	Tuesday	Wednesday	Thursday	Friday	Saturday	Sunday		Total weekly health points
___ pt. +	___ pt. +	___ pt. +	___ pt. +	___ pt. +	___ pt. +	___ pt.	=	___ pt. (100 pt. maximum)

INTERPRETING THE EFFECTIVENESS OF YOUR WEEKLY EXERCISE EFFORT*

100 health points from exercise	Ideal. *You couldn't do better!*
70-99 health points from exercise	Very good. *Be proud of yourself.*
50-69 health points from exercise	Good. *But you could do better.*
20-49 health points from exercise	Fair. *Try a bit harder.*
10-19 health points from exercise	Poor. *But it's better than nothing.*
Less than 10 health points from exercise	Very poor. *Come on, now.*

*If your breathing disorder or other conditions are such that you are unable to attain the desired weekly number of health points, please ignore this interpretation. Be proud of whatever progress you are able to make.

System gives you a way to chart your progress in black and white so that you can see what you are accomplishing.

Our Health Points System should be used only by those of you whose breathlessness is no more severe than Grade 3. It's not intended for people with breathing problems more severe than that. Moreover, if you have a Grade 3 disability, be satisfied with 50 health points per week.

If you have severe breathlessness that places you in Grade 3 or 4 and you find that you cannot attain the desired weekly number of health points, don't worry or become discouraged. If you perform some type of aerobic exercise—even an exercise for which I don't provide health points charts—for a minimum of 15 minutes at least 3 days a week, you'll derive important health benefits. Rather than trying to fulfill unrealistic expectations, be proud of what progress you are able to make. Also, remember that the effectiveness categories in the Weekly Health Points Exercise Tally Sheet are not applicable to persons whose breathing disorder severity—as opposed to factors such as a lack of interest or desire—prevents them from attaining the recommended weekly health points.

HOW TO UTILIZE
THE HEALTH POINTS CHARTS

The only way to accurately measure energy expenditure during exercise is through laboratory testing. There, technicians use sophisticated equipment to measure the exact amount of oxygen the body takes up during a workout. The charts at the end of this chapter (Tables 4.1-4.5) are derived from numerous exercise research studies performed in such laboratories.

Tables 4.1 to 4.4 list health points for walking, jogging, stationary cycling (legs only), and the Schwinn Air-Dyne (all of which were described in chapter 3). We were able to formulate charts for these forms of exercise because none require much skill and considerable outstanding research data are available on them.

Be aware that carrying or pulling portable oxygen along with you while you walk increases your energy expenditure. If you do so, add 15% to your walking health points score to compensate for this. (To add 15%, simply multiply your score by 1.15.)

If you exercise on equipment that gives you a readout of the calories you've expended, you can easily convert that number to health points.

First, obtain your conversion number by dividing your body weight in pounds by 11, or by dividing your body weight in kilograms by 5. Divide the readout number by your conversion number. For example, if the readout number is 120 calories and you weigh 165 pounds (75 kilograms), you've earned 8 health points (165 pounds/11 = 75 kilograms/5 = 15 and 120 calories/15 = 8 health points).

To determine the health points you earn for walking or jogging, you need to know the distance you covered during your workout (to convert kilometers to miles, divide by 1.6) and the time it took you. If you have access to a measured running track, figuring the distance will pose no problem. Otherwise, you might want to invest in a pedometer or use your car's odometer to stake out a stretch of road to use as a track. You'll need a stopwatch or a watch with a second hand to accurately time your exercise session.

To find your health points for stationary cycling or the Schwinn Air-Dyne, you'll need to know the duration of your workout, your work rate (wattage) or work load (for the Schwinn Air-Dyne), and your weight (to convert kilograms to pounds, multiply by 2.2).

To show you how easy the Health Points System is to use, an example from Dave Saxon's training diary is on page 68, which shows the number of health points he earned for each activity. At the time, he was in his 20th week of training and weighed 165 pounds (about 75 kilograms).

These workouts enabled Dave to exceed our minimum weekly recommended goal of 50 health points.

OTHER AEROBIC EXERCISE CHOICES: THE PROS AND CONS

Table 4.5 provides information on how to calculate health points for other aerobic activities. To vary your routine, you may want to try some of these forms of exercise. These activities either require skill, are influenced by external factors such as the weather or terrain, or have not been adequately researched. So although these charts are useful, they aren't as precise as those for walking, jogging, and stationary cycling. To use this table you need to know how long you exercised and whether you exercised at a light (RPE or RPB < 3), moderate (RPE or RPB = 3), or heavy (RPE or RPB > 3) intensity.

Your ideal aerobic exercise has five basic characteristics:

- It's pleasant. You're more likely to stick with an exercise you enjoy.

Date	Activity	Time	Distance/ work load	Health points	Notes
S					
M	Walk	22-1/2 min	1 mile	6.8	*Lots of smog outside today.*
	Schwinn Air-Dyne	22-1/2 min	1 WL	9	
T					
W	Walk	20 min	.9 miles	5.7	*No problems.*
	Cycle (legs)	25 min	50 watts	10.5	
T					
F	Walk	20 min	.8 miles	5.7	*I took it easy today.*
	Schwinn Air-Dyne	20 min	1 WL	8	
S	Swim	20 min	3 RPE	8.8	*Wish I could get to the pool more often!*
				54.5	**Total: Week** 20

- It is practical and fits into your lifestyle. It's something you can do conveniently year-round.
- It uses large muscle groups. The larger the muscle groups you exercise, the greater your body's oxygen uptake will be for a given ventilatory requirement.

- It is applicable to the physical demands of your life, in accordance with the specificity of exercise principle. For example, if you use your bike to commute to work or to do errands, cycling would be an important exercise choice. Walking would be a good choice if you live in a city and need to walk a lot to get around.
- For patients who have exercise-induced asthma, it does not precipitate this condition.

Here are the pros and cons of some specific aerobic exercises that weren't covered in the last chapter. There are many other choices as well; the following are some of the more popular exercises.

Swimming

This is an excellent aerobic activity because it uses both the upper and lower body muscles. And because it's a non-weight-bearing activity, the chances of a musculoskeletal injury are low. Swimming is especially valuable for people with lower back problems or arthritis. And for reasons you'll learn about in the next chapter, it's one of the activities least likely to trigger exercise-induced asthma.[2]

If you're overweight, shedding pounds through exercise should be a goal. But swimming may not help you as much in this regard as some other forms of aerobic exercise.[3] Although the precise reason for this is not known, it may be because swimming causes less rise in body temperature than do other aerobic activities.

Aqua-Aerobics

This is just what the name implies—aerobic exercises done in water. The advantages and disadvantages of this increasingly popular low-impact sport are similar to those for swimming. Those of you who find the prospect of exercising in a swimming pool appealing can consult Ken Cooper's book *Overcoming Hypertension* for detailed guidelines.[4]

Cross-Country Skiing

Ken Cooper rates this as the top aerobic activity. He reasons, "You have more muscles involved than just the legs; and any time you get more muscles involved, you get more aerobic benefit."[1] And the heavy clothing you wear and the weighty equipment you must carry further enhance the aerobic effect (or energy expenditure) over that of walking or jogging at similar speeds.

There are drawbacks, though. The total exertion is greatly affected by variations in skill, snow surface, terrain, temperature and weather conditions, and altitude. Also, it's difficult to take your pulse in the middle of this activity. If you're prone to exercise-induced asthma, the cold, dry air may set off an attack.[5] You may prefer to use mechanical cross-country skiing devices, which some of our patients enjoy. They enable you to burn calories efficiently and provide a low-impact activity that's unlikely to cause musculoskeletal problems.

Stair Climbing

Stair-climbing machines always seem to be in use at health clubs. These machines simulate the act of climbing flights of stairs, enabling you to work the large muscles in your back, buttocks, and legs and to expend large amounts of energy quickly. Because stair climbing is strenuous and may cause a marked increase in ventilatory require-ments, heart rate, and blood pressure, it's generally not an appropriate activity for people with significant COPD or cardiovascular disease. Nor is it a good way for beginners to start an exercise program. If you decide to try stair climbing, wait until you've been working out for at least 8 weeks before adding it to your exercise regimen.[6]

People with knee problems should probably find another way to get an aerobic workout. The stress stair climbing places on the knee joint is thought to be equivalent to lifting four to six times your body weight. Needless to say, it's likely to aggravate existing problems in that area.[6]

Rope Skipping

This is a practical, enjoyable, and easily accessible aerobic activity. But it's not a popular choice, because it's relatively strenuous and it may result in excessively high ventilatory requirements and heart rates. Even at that, for a given ventilatory requirement or heart rate, the energy expenditure is not as high as that for some other strenuous aerobic exercises, such as jogging. And rope skipping exposes you to the risk of musculoskeletal disorders—a significant drawback.

Aerobic Dance

Aerobic dancing is steady, rhythmic movements done to the beat of relatively fast music, usually rock. Recently benches that range in height from 6 to 12 inches (15 to 30 centimeters) have been introduced into aerobic dance workouts to increase the exercise intensity while reducing the impact and risk of injury.[7] People who have episodic asthma and enjoy aerobic dance have been able to improve their fitness via these step aerobics workouts. But I cannot recommend this for people with severe COPD or cardiovascular disease unless the class is especially designed for them (and, frankly, I don't know of many). Aerobic dancing is strenuous and would probably cause such people to become out of breath and exceed their training heart rate limit.

Circuit Resistance Training

This is a combination of aerobics and muscle strengthening. Typically an exerciser uses a series of resistance-training machines and moves from one to the next with very short rest periods—usually 15 to 30 seconds—in between. Performed correctly, circuit training improves the cardiovascular system, builds and tones muscles, and burns calories during one carefully constructed workout.

Sounds great, doesn't it? I didn't want to dismiss this exercise option out of hand, so I reviewed the medical literature and did my own study of its possible rehabilitation benefits.[8] Here's the catch: The primary benefit is enhancement of muscular strength, not energy expenditure. So I do not recommend it for people with breathing problems unless it's performed in conjunction with other forms of aerobic exercise.

It's best that people with severe COPD or cardiovascular disease avoid circuit resistance training unless they've got professional supervision and guidance. Even then, the increase in lactic acid production that usually accompanies circuit training may cause extreme breathlessness.

Recreational Sports

People with episodic asthma who have no other serious chronic diseases can participate in, and excel at, just about any exercise or sport. But people with COPD should be aware that many sports, particularly when they turn competitive, involve sudden bursts of high-intensity exercise that may not be good for them. They cause a steep increase in ventilatory requirements and also predispose

Other aerobic choices

susceptible people to cardiac complications. If you engage in recreational sports, you may have to modify the rules to minimize the competitive aspects and avoid those sudden spurts of high exertion. Doing this will help keep your RPE, RPB, and heart rate within the designated limits. When performed in such a way, recreational sports can be, and often are, a valuable part of a pulmonary rehabilitation exercise program.

Although I have not included sample introductory programs for each of these alternative exercise choices, you can use the walking and stationary cycling programs at the end of chapter 3 as a blueprint from which to plan your own. For example, an introductory swimming program might be as follows on page 73.

When using this swimming program—as with any aerobic exercise—start at a comfortable intensity. During the initial weeks, do not exceed 85% of your maximal heart rate and an RPE or RPB of 5. Also, warm up and cool down for at least 5 minutes each. You can do this by swimming slower or doing other activities in the water.

Week	Duration per session	Frequency per week
1	2.5 minutes	3-5 times
2	5 minutes	3-5 times
3	7.5 minutes	3-5 times
4	10 minutes	3-5 times
5	12.5 minutes	3-5 times
6	15 minutes	3-5 times
7	17.5 minutes	3-5 times
8	20 minutes	3-5 times
9	25 minutes	3-5 times
10	30 minutes	3-5 times
11 and onward	It's time to start earning those 50 to 100 health points a week. Keep your exercise time at 30 minutes per session and gradually increase your swimming speed until you exceed 60% of your maximal heart rate (if you are not doing so yet). If this does not result in the desired weekly energy expenditure using the Other Aerobic Activities chart (Table 4.5, pp. 82-84), do one or more of the following: Try exercising within the upper range of your target heart rate zone; exercise more frequently; or increase the duration of each exercise session.	

THE FOUR-LETTER WORD
YOU MUST NOT UTTER

That word is *quit*.

You've probably noticed I keep emphasizing *regular* exercise—not sporadic exercise, not fair-weather exercise, but the kind of persistent exercise you engage in almost daily because it's a habit, like brushing your teeth. There's a reason. When you exercise, your body and its organ systems are exposed to potent physiological stimuli. If you exercise regularly at an appropriate intensity and duration, these stimuli result in specific adaptations that both enhance your ability to exercise and improve your health. In other words, you'll receive all the benefits of a physically active lifestyle (benefits I outlined in chapter 2).

Unfortunately, these benefits can't be stored up for a rainy day. They're reversible. All it takes to set this backtracking in motion is abstinence. If you stop training or reduce your physical activity to below your required level, your body's systems soon readjust themselves to this diminished amount of physiological stimuli. The result: Those hard-won, exercise-related gains, which you worked so long and hard to achieve, are lost.

This reversibility concept is best epitomized by a landmark study of 16,936 Harvard University alumni by Dr. Ralph S. Paffenbarger, Jr., and his colleagues.[9] In this study, many former college athletes became inactive adults. Consequently, they were in worse shape—and at greater risk for cardiovascular disease—than their contemporaries who had not participated in college sports but had started exercising later in life. Researchers do not know how long it takes after you stop training before all the health benefits of exercise are lost. We do know that even after many years of training, fitness declines rapidly during the first 12 to 21 days of inactivity. And the fitness benefits of regular exercise are almost totally lost after about 2 or 3 months.[10]

In view of this, it's imperative that you stick with your exercise program once you get started. But this is easier said than done. Several studies on exercise compliance have shown that half or more of all patients drop out of their exercise program within 6 months and that the critical dropout period is the first 3 months or so. You need motivators to get you through this critical time. The following suggestions will help keep you exercising even when you'd rather be home in bed or watching television.

• *Make sure you fully understand the costs of not exercising versus the benefits of exercising.*

• *Start exercising slowly and progress gradually.* If you follow the beginning programs outlined in this book, you'll be doing just that.

• *Choose a form of exercise that's convenient as well as enjoyable.* If you constantly score below a "4" on the Enjoyment Rating checklist in the Daily Exercise Training Log at the end of chapter 3, your exercise program needs to be modified.

• *Find a role model*—a friend, relative, or acquaintance who leads a physically active life. Find out why that person loves exercise.

• *Learn from your past exercise experiences.* Try to figure out where you went wrong previously.

• *Obtain as much support for your exercise program as possible.* Enlist the company—or at least the moral support—of those closest to you. Health promotion should be a family affair. After all, your relatives are also at risk for developing such chronic illnesses as heart disease. Explain this to your family and use it as the rationale to get as many of them as possible involved in your exercise program. In more ways than one, you're all in this together.

On the other hand, never let peer pressure force you to exercise more strenuously than you should. Although exercising with others has many advantages, always work at your own pace. You've got a special condition—a breathing disorder—and even if your exercise companion has one, too, his or her case isn't necessarily the same as yours. Goals are important exercise motivators, but keep yours realistic and modify them continually as your condition changes.

• *Bring your body to your place of exercise, even if your mind is temporarily on strike.* Often it's just a matter of overcoming mental inertia. A body at rest prefers to remain at rest, no doubt. But once you start exercising, you may find you enjoy it more than you anticipated. Remember, special occasions, such as holidays or vacations, are no excuse.

• *Finally, remember that exercise is forever.* Physical activity is a lifelong pursuit.

I urge you to do everything in your power to keep from becoming an exercise dropout, especially during the crucial initial months. Once you've passed the 6-month mark and tasted some of the tantalizing benefits of an active lifestyle, there's less and less chance you'll ever revert back to unhealthy inactivity.

Exercise dropout rate

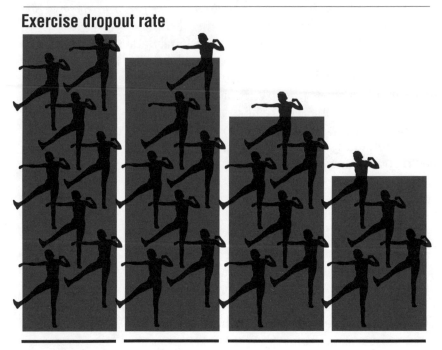

| January | March | April | July |

Table 4.1
Walking Health Points Chart

Time (min:sec)	Distance (miles)	Health points	Time (min:sec)	Distance (miles)	Health points
5:00	Under 0.10	0.8	7:30	Under 0.15	1.3
	0.10-0.14	1.0		0.15-0.19	1.5
	0.15-0.19	1.2		0.20-0.24	1.7
	0.20-0.24	1.4		0.25-0.29	1.9
	0.25-0.29	1.6		0.30-0.34	2.1
	0.30-0.33	1.8		0.35-0.39	2.3
	Over 0.33	*		0.40-0.44	2.5
				0.45-0.49	2.7
				Over 0.49	*
10:00	Under 0.20	1.7	12:30	Under 0.20	1.9
	0.20-0.24	1.8		0.20-0.29	2.3
	0.25-0.29	2.0		0.30-0.39	2.7
	0.30-0.34	2.2		0.40-0.49	3.1
	0.35-0.39	2.4		0.50-0.59	3.5
	0.40-0.44	2.6		0.60-0.69	3.9
	0.45-0.49	2.8		0.70-0.79	4.3
	0.50-0.54	3.0		0.80-0.83	4.7
	0.55-0.59	3.2		Over 0.83	*
	0.60-0.66	3.6			
	Over 0.66	*			
15:00	Under 0.30	2.5	17:30	Under 0.30	2.8
	0.30-0.39	2.9		0.30-0.49	3.5
	0.40-0.49	3.3		0.50-0.69	4.3
	0.50-0.59	3.7		0.70-0.89	5.1
	0.60-0.69	4.1		0.90-1.09	5.9
	0.70-0.79	4.5		1.10-1.16	6.7
	0.80-0.89	4.9		Over 1.16	*
	0.90-0.99	5.3			
	Over 0.99	*			
20:00	Under 0.40	3.4	22:30	Under 0.40	3.6
	0.40-0.59	4.1		0.40-0.59	4.4
	0.60-0.79	4.9		0.60-0.79	5.2
	0.80-0.99	5.7		0.80-0.99	6.0
	1.00-1.19	6.5		1.00-1.19	6.8
	1.20-1.33	7.3		1.20-1.39	7.6
	Over 1.33	*		1.40-1.49	8.4
				Over 1.49	*
25:00	Under 0.50	4.2	27:30	Under 0.50	4.5
	0.50-0.69	5.0		0.50-0.69	5.2
	0.70-0.89	5.8		0.70-0.89	6.0
	0.90-1.09	6.6		0.90-1.09	6.8

(Cont.)

Table 4.1
(Continued)

Time (min:sec)	Distance (miles)	Health points	Time (min:sec)	Distance (miles)	Health points
25:00 (Cont.)			27:30 (Cont.)		
	1.10-1.29	7.4		1.10-1.29	7.6
	1.30-1.49	8.2		1.30-1.49	8.4
	1.50-1.66	9.0		1.50-1.69	9.2
	Over 1.66	*		1.70-1.83	10.0
				Over 1.83	*
30:00	Under 0.50	4.6	35:00	Under 0.75	6.1
	0.50-0.74	5.6		0.75-0.99	7.0
	0.75-0.99	6.6		1.00-1.24	8.0
	1.00-1.24	7.6		1.25-1.49	9.0
	1.25-1.49	8.6		1.50-1.74	10.0
	1.50-1.74	9.6		1.75-1.99	11.0
	1.75-1.99	10.6		2.00-2.24	12.0
	Over 1.99	*		2.25-2.33	13.0
				Over 2.33	*
40:00	Under 1.00	7.5	45:00	Under 1.00	7.9
	1.00-1.24	8.5		1.00-1.49	9.9
	1.25-1.49	9.5		1.50-1.99	11.9
	1.50-1.74	10.5		2.00-2.49	13.9
	1.75-1.99	11.5		2.50-2.99	15.9
	2.00-2.24	12.5		Over 2.99	*
	2.25-2.49	13.5			
	2.50-2.66	14.5			
	Over 2.66	*			
50:00	Under 1.00	8.4	55:00	Under 1.00	8.8
	1.00-1.49	10.3		1.00-1.49	10.8
	1.50-1.99	12.4		1.50-1.99	12.8
	2.00-2.49	14.4		2.00-2.49	14.8
	2.50-2.99	16.4		2.50-2.99	16.8
	3.00-3.33	18.4		3.00-3.49	18.8
	Over 3.33	*		3.50-3.66	20.8
				Over 3.66	*
60:00	Under 1.00	9.3			
	1.00-1.49	11.2			
	1.50-1.99	13.2			
	2.00-2.49	15.2			
	2.50-2.99	17.2			
	3.00-3.49	19.2			
	3.50-3.99	21.2			
	Over 3.99	*			

*Use the Jogging Health Points Chart (Table 4.2).

Table 4.2
Jogging Health Points Chart

Time (min:sec)	Distance (miles)	Health points	Time (min:sec)	Distance (miles)	Health points
5:00	Under 0.40	3.6	7:30	Under 0.50	4.7
	0.40-0.49	4.4		0.50-0.59	5.4
	0.50-0.59	5.2		0.60-0.69	6.2
	0.60-0.69	6.0		0.70-0.79	7.0
	Over 0.69	6.8		0.80-0.89	7.8
				0.90-0.99	8.6
				1.00-1.09	9.4
				Over 1.09	10.2
10:00	Under 0.80	7.3	12:30	Under 1.00	9.2
	0.80-0.89	8.0		1.00-1.19	10.7
	0.90-0.99	8.8		1.20-1.39	12.3
	1.00-1.09	9.6		1.40-1.59	13.9
	1.10-1.19	10.4		1.60-1.79	15.5
	1.20-1.29	11.2		Over 1.79	17.1
	1.30-1.39	12.0			
	1.40-1.49	12.8			
	Over 1.49	13.6			
15:00	Under 1.20	10.9	17:30	Under 1.40	12.8
	1.20-1.39	12.5		1.40-1.59	14.3
	1.40-1.59	14.1		1.60-1.79	15.9
	1.60-1.79	15.7		1.80-1.99	17.5
	1.80-1.99	17.3		2.00-2.19	19.1
	2.00-2.19	18.9		2.20-2.39	20.7
	Over 2.19	20.5		2.40-2.59	22.4
				Over 2.59	24.0
20:00	Under 1.50	13.8	22:30	Under 1.75	16.0
	1.50-1.74	15.7		1.75-1.99	18.0
	1.75-1.99	17.7		2.00-2.24	20.0
	2.00-2.24	19.7		2.25-2.49	22.0
	2.25-2.49	21.7		2.50-2.74	24.0
	2.50-2.74	23.7		2.75-2.99	26.0
	2.75-2.99	25.7		3.00-3.24	28.0
	Over 2.99	27.7		Over 3.24	30.0
25:00	Under 2.00	18.2	27:30	Under 2.00	18.5
	2.00-2.24	20.2		2.00-2.24	20.4
	2.25-2.49	22.2		2.25-2.49	22.4
	2.50-2.74	24.2		2.50-2.74	24.4
	2.75-2.99	26.2		2.75-2.99	26.4
	3.00-3.24	28.2		3.00-3.24	28.4
	3.25-3.49	30.2		3.25-3.49	30.4

(Cont.)

Table 4.2
(Continued)

Time (min:sec)	Distance (miles)	Health points	Time (min:sec)	Distance (miles)	Health points
25:00 (Cont.)			27:30 (Cont.)		
	3.50-3.74	32.2		3.50-3.74	32.5
	Over 3.74	34.2		3.75-3.99	34.5
				Over 3.99	36.5
30:00	Under 2.50	22.7	35:00	Under 2.75	25.1
	2.50-2.74	24.6		2.75-2.99	27.0
	2.75-2.99	26.6		3.00-3.24	29.1
	3.00-3.24	28.6		3.25-3.49	31.1
	3.25-3.49	30.6		3.50-3.74	33.1
	3.50-3.74	32.6		3.75-3.99	35.1
	3.75-3.99	34.6		4.00-4.24	37.1
	4.00-4.24	36.6		4.25-4.49	39.1
	Over 4.24	38.6		4.50-4.74	41.1
				4.75-4.99	43.1
				Over 4.99	45.1
40:00	Under 3.00	27.6	45:00	Under 3.50	32.0
	3.00-3.49	31.5		3.50-3.99	35.9
	3.50-3.99	35.5		4.00-4.49	40.0
	4.00-4.49	39.5		4.50-4.99	44.0
	4.50-4.99	43.5		5.00-5.49	48.0
	5.00-5.49	47.5		5.50-5.99	52.0
	5.50-5.99	51.6		6.00-6.49	56.0
	Over 5.99	55.6		Over 6.49	60.0
50:00	Under 4.00	36.5	55:00	Under 4.50	40.9
	4.00-4.49	40.4		4.50-4.99	44.8
	4.50-4.99	44.4		5.00-5.49	48.9
	5.00-5.49	48.4		5.50-5.99	52.9
	5.50-5.99	52.4		6.00-6.49	56.9
	6.00-6.49	56.4		6.50-6.99	60.9
	6.50-6.99	60.4		7.00-7.49	64.9
	7.00-7.49	64.5		7.50-7.99	68.9
	Over 7.49	68.5		Over 7.99	72.9
60:00	Under 4.50	41.3			
	4.50-4.99	45.3			
	5.00-5.49	49.3			
	5.50-5.99	53.3			
	6.00-6.49	57.3			
	6.50-6.99	61.3			
	7.00-7.49	65.3			
	7.50-7.99	69.3			
	8.00-8.49	73.4			
	8.50-8.99	77.4			
	Over 8.99	81.4			

Table 4.3
Stationary Cycling (Legs Only) Health Points Chart

Work rate (watts)	Under 100 lb	100 to 124 lb	125 to 149 lb	150 to 174 lb	175 to 199 lb	200 to 224 lb	225 to 249 lb	Over 249 lb
				Health points per minute				
Under 25	0.34	0.28	0.24	0.22	0.20	0.18	0.17	0.16
25-49	0.54	0.44	0.36	0.32	0.28	0.26	0.24	0.22
50-74	0.76	0.60	0.50	0.42	0.38	0.34	0.32	0.30
75-99	0.98	0.76	0.62	0.54	0.48	0.42	0.38	0.36
100-124	1.20	0.92	0.76	0.64	0.56	0.50	0.46	0.42
125-149	1.42	1.10	0.90	0.76	0.66	0.58	0.54	0.48
150-174	1.64	1.26	1.02	0.86	0.76	0.68	0.60	0.56
175-199	1.86	1.42	1.16	0.98	0.84	0.76	0.68	0.62
200-224	2.08	1.58	1.28	1.08	0.94	0.84	0.76	0.68
225-249	2.30	1.76	1.42	1.20	1.04	0.92	0.82	0.76
Over 249	2.52	1.92	1.56	1.30	1.14	1.00	0.90	0.82

Table 4.4
Schwinn Air-Dyne Health Points Chart

Work load	Under 100 lb	100 to 124 lb	125 to 149 lb	150 to 174 lb	175 to 199 lb	200 to 224 lb	225 to 249 lb	Over 249 lb
				Health points per minute				
Under 0.5	0.34	0.28	0.24	0.22	0.20	0.18	0.17	0.16
0.5-0.9	0.52	0.40	0.34	0.30	0.26	0.24	0.22	0.21
1.0-1.4	0.74	0.56	0.48	0.40	0.36	0.32	0.30	0.28
1.5-1.9	0.96	0.74	0.60	0.52	0.46	0.42	0.38	0.34
2.0-2.4	1.18	0.90	0.74	0.62	0.56	0.50	0.44	0.42
2.5-2.9	1.40	1.06	0.86	0.74	0.64	0.58	0.52	0.48
3.0-3.4	1.62	1.22	1.00	0.84	0.74	0.66	0.60	0.54
3.5-3.9	1.84	1.40	1.14	0.96	0.84	0.74	0.66	0.62
4.0-4.4	2.06	1.56	1.26	1.06	0.92	0.82	0.74	0.68
4.5-4.9	2.28	1.72	1.40	1.18	1.02	0.90	0.82	0.74
Over 4.9	2.50	1.88	1.52	1.28	1.12	0.98	0.88	0.80

Table 4.5
Other Aerobic Activities

| Activity | Health points per minute | | |
| | Intensity* | | |
	Light	Moderate	Heavy
Aerobic dancing	0.35	0.53	0.79
Alpine skiing	0.35	0.53	0.70
Aqua-aerobics	0.35	0.53	0.79
Arm-cycle ergometry	0.22	0.35	0.61
Backpacking	0.53	0.70	0.88
(5% slope, 44 lb or 20 kg)			
4.0 mph (6.4 kph)	0.70		
4.5 mph (7.2 kph)	0.84		
5.0 mph (8.0 kph)	1.02		
6.0 mph (9.6 kph)	1.15		
7.0 mph (11.2 kph)	1.36		
Badminton	0.26	0.53	0.79
Ballet	0.44	0.53	0.70
Ballroom dancing	0.26	0.35	0.44
Baseball	0.26	0.35	0.44
Basketball	0.53	0.70	0.96
Bicycling	0.26	0.61	0.88
6.3 mph (10 kph)	0.42		
9.4 mph (15 kph)	0.52		
12.5 mph (20 kph)	0.62		
15.6 mph (25 kph)	0.74		
18.8 mph (30 kph)	0.86		
Canoeing	0.26	0.35	0.53
Catch (ball)	0.26	0.35	0.44
Circuit resistance training	0.26	0.44	0.61
Cricket	0.26	0.35	0.44
Cross-country skiing	0.44	0.79	1.14
2.5 mph (4 kph)	0.48		
3.8 mph (6 kph)	0.67		
5.0 mph (8 kph)	0.87		
6.3 mph (10 kph)	1.07		
7.5 mph (12 kph)	1.25		
8.8 mph (14 kph)	1.44		
Exercise classes	0.35	0.53	0.79
Fencing	0.44	0.61	0.88
Field hockey	0.53	0.70	0.88
Figure skating	0.35	0.53	0.88
Football (American)	0.44	0.53	0.61
Football (touch)	0.44	0.53	0.70

Table 4.5
(Continued)

Activity	Health points per minute		
		Intensity*	
	Light	Moderate	Heavy
Golf			
Carrying clubs	0.45		
Pulling cart	0.35		
Riding cart	0.22		
Gymnastics	0.44	0.61	0.88
Handball (4-wall)	0.53	0.70	0.96
Hiking	0.26	0.53	0.70
Home calisthenics	0.26	0.44	0.70
Hunting	0.26	0.44	0.61
Ice hockey	0.53	0.70	0.88
Judo	0.53	0.70	1.05
Karate	0.44	0.70	1.05
Kayaking	0.53	0.70	0.96
7.8 mph (12.5 kph)	0.68		
9.4 mph (15.0 kph)	0.96		
Lacrosse	0.53	0.70	0.88
Modern dancing	0.44	0.53	0.70
Mountaineering	0.61	0.70	0.88
Orienteering	0.70	0.88	1.05
Racquetball	0.53	0.79	1.05
Rebounding	0.31	0.44	0.53
Rollerskating	0.44	0.57	0.70
Rope skipping	0.61	0.88	1.05
66 per min	0.86		
84 per min	0.92		
100 per min	0.96		
120 per min	1.00		
125 per min	1.02		
130 per min	1.03		
135 per min	1.05		
145 per min	1.06		
Rowing	0.61	0.88	1.14
2.5 mph (4 kph)	0.48		
5.0 mph (8 kph)	0.90		
7.5 mph (12 kph)	1.18		
10.0 mph (16 kph)	1.44		
12.5 mph (20 kph)	1.67		

(Cont.)

Table 4.5
(Continued)

Activity		Health points per minute		
			Intensity*	
		Light	Moderate	Heavy
Rugby		0.53	0.70	0.96
Scuba diving		0.35	0.44	0.53
Sculling		0.35	0.53	0.88
Skateboarding		0.44	0.57	0.70
Skating (ice)		0.35	0.61	1.14
11.3 mph (18 kph)	0.35			
15.6 mph (25 kph)	0.42			
17.5 mph (28 kph)	0.81			
20.0 mph (32 kph)	0.95			
22.5 mph (36 kph)	1.33			
Snorkeling		0.35	0.44	0.53
Soccer		0.44	0.61	0.96
Softball		0.26	0.35	0.44
Squash		0.53	0.79	1.05
Stair climbing		0.35	0.61	0.96
Swimming (beach)		0.18	0.26	0.35
Swimming (pool)		0.26	0.44	0.79
1.3 mph (2 kph)	0.38			
1.6 mph (2.5 kph)	0.60			
1.9 mph (3.0 kph)	0.78			
2.2 mph (3.5 kph)	1.01			
2.5 mph (4.0 kph)	1.19			
Synchronized swimming		0.35	0.53	0.70
Table tennis		0.26	0.44	0.70
Tennis		0.35	0.53	0.88
Volleyball		0.44	0.53	0.70
Walking up stairs		0.35	0.53	0.70
Water polo		0.53	0.70	0.96
Wrestling		0.53	0.79	1.05

*Light intensity results in minimal perspiration and only a slight increase in breathing above normal (RPE or RPB of less than 3). Moderate intensity results in definite perspiration and above normal breathing (RPE or RPB of 3). Heavy intensity corresponds to heavy perspiration and breathing (RPE or RPB of more than 3). These values are adapted from an expert committee report of the Canada Fitness Survey - source M. Jette et al., Clinical Cardiology, 13 (1990): 555-565.

Chapter 4
Prescription

❏ If you're a novice exerciser, consider using one of my beginning exercise programs. Ask your doctor to help you adapt it to suit the medical realities of your particular breathing disorder.

❏ Use the Health Points System to gain optimal health benefits with minimal risk.

❏ Do not attempt to earn your quota of health points in fewer than three workouts, on at least 3 separate days, each week.

❏ When using the Health Points System, modulate the frequency, intensity, and duration of your exercise to earn 50 to 100 health points each week.

❏ Keep your goals realistic, and modify them continually as your condition permits.

❏ If your condition is such that you cannot attain the desired weekly health points, don't become discouraged. If you perform some type of aerobic exercise for a minimum of 15 minutes at least 3 days a week, you'll derive important health benefits.

❏ Be proud of whatever progress you are able to make.

❏ Do everything in your power to keep from becoming an exercise dropout, especially during the crucial initial months.

Chapter 5

Safety First: Essential Exercise Guidelines for People With Respiratory Ailments

Fortunately, much of the guesswork has been eliminated from prescribing exercise as therapy for people with breathing disorders. Today, well-informed physicians can prescribe exercise just as they would medications. However, as with drugs, certain precautions are needed to make sure your exercise regimen is both safe and effective.

Even healthy exercisers should follow certain general safety guidelines. These guidelines have been described in detail in other books from the Cooper Clinic, such as *Running Without Fear*,[1] *The Aerobics Program for Total Well-Being*,[2] and *The New Aerobics for Women*.[3] In this chapter, I'll focus on the special problems and hazards associated with exercise for respiratory disease patients.

TEN SAFE-EXERCISE GUIDELINES

The following safety guidelines are intended to reduce the chances that exercise will exacerbate your condition. They're also designed to help prevent exercise-related cardiac complications and musculo-skeletal injuries. I encourage you to follow them as well as to listen to the advice of your doctor.

EXERCISE SAFETY GUIDELINE 1

Don't even think about beginning exercise until your breathing problem has been stabilized through appropriate medical treatment.

People with COPD need medication to control their respiratory condition. It would be foolish to begin an exercise program before you've done whatever is possible, medically, to correct any reversible airway obstruction you have.[4]

But if you have only mild episodic asthma, you may be able to manage your problem with nondrug approaches. For example, if you know what triggers an asthma attack, avoid that thing or activity when reasonably possible. If exercise is the precipitating factor, don't write it off as something you can no longer do. Exercise is still possible—indeed, desirable—for all the reasons I outlined in chapter 2. (I'll tell you how to work with your episodic asthma condition later in this chapter.)

EXERCISE SAFETY GUIDELINE 2

Have a thorough medical evaluation before starting your exercise program, and at regular intervals thereafter.

Everyone with a respiratory ailment needs to have a complete medical exam and obtain his or her doctor's permission before beginning our health points exercise program. This is true even if, in your opinion, your condition is stable or you have only mild episodic asthma.[5] For a summary of what you can expect during a thorough pre-exercise screening checkup, see Appendix B.

For some of you, the risks of exercise may outweigh the benefits. Your doctor's permission to exercise will depend primarily on the type and severity of your breathing disorder and whether any complications have arisen because of it. Also, you need to know whether you have other chronic diseases that will restrict your capacity for exertion. These conditions are listed in the following checklist.

✓ **Do *NOT* Exercise if Your Physician Indicates You Have Any of These Conditions** ✓

Ask your doctor if you have any of the following. If you do, avoid aerobic exercise until therapy or the passage of time controls or corrects the condition.

_____ Unstable angina pectoris or a recent severe heart attack

_____ Recent significant change in resting ECG that has not been adequately investigated and managed

_____ A recent embolism

_____ Thrombophlebitis or an intracardiac thrombus

_____ Active or suspected myocarditis or pericarditis

_____ Acute or inadequately controlled heart failure

_____ Moderate to severe aortic stenosis

_____ Clinically significant hypertrophic obstructive cardiomyopathy

_____ Suspected or known aneurysm—cardiac or vascular—that your physician believes may be worsened by exercise

_____ Theophylline toxicity (Theophylline is a bronchodilator drug often used to treat breathing disorders.)

_____ Uncontrolled atrial or ventricular arrhythmias that are considered to be clinically significant

_____ Resting heart rate greater than 120 beats per minute

_____ Third-degree heart block

_____ Uncontrolled hypertension with resting systolic blood pressure above 200 mmHg or diastolic blood pressure above 120 mmHg

_____ Recent fall in systolic blood pressure of more than 20 mmHg that was not caused by medication

_____ Uncontrolled metabolic disease, such as diabetes mellitus, thyrotoxicosis, or myxedema

_____ Acute infection or fever

_____ Chronic infectious disease—such as mononucleosis, hepatitis, or AIDS—that your doctor believes may be worsened by exercise

_____ Significant electrolyte disturbances

_____ Major emotional distress (psychosis)

_____ Neuromuscular, musculoskeletal, or rheumatoid disorders that may be made worse by exercise, in your physician's opinion

_____ Pregnancy complications

_____ Any other condition known to preclude exercise

Note. From American College of Sports Medicine: Guidelines for Exercise Testing and Prescription, 4th edition. Philadelphia: Lea and Febiger, 1991. Adapted with permission.

Of course, your pre-exercise medical exam won't be your last. Periodic checkups are important because respiratory ailments are often progressive. Over time, your lung function may deteriorate further, new complications may develop, or existing ones may worsen. The course that your condition takes cannot be predicted with 100% certainty. Nor can anyone guess the exact impact that regular exercise will have on your body.

The central principle of pulmonary rehabilitation is that therapeutic decisions must be continually modified based on each patient's response. That's why I think an evaluation after 12 weeks on an exercise program is important for beginning exercisers. It gives your physician the opportunity to alter your exercise regimen, if necessary, and to reassess any problems with your therapy. In addition to a physical examination and a discussion with your doctor, this follow-up checkup should include a repeat exercise test (see Appendix B). Further tests are at your doctor's discretion.

Provided no disturbing abnormalities are detected, such exercise-related checkups can be annual thereafter. But if you notice disturbing symptoms at any time between regularly scheduled doctor visits, do not hesitate to get an immediate appointment to have them looked into.

EXERCISE SAFETY GUIDELINE 3

Find out whether you need direct medical supervision when you exercise—and whether it's only during the early weeks of the program or on a permanent basis.

A breathing problem shouldn't keep you from doing carefully tailored range-of-motion and muscle-strengthening exercises. But for some of you, aerobic exercise may be too risky. For others, aerobic exercise may be possible, *but only under special supervised conditions.* A *medically supervised* exercise program is one in which a doctor or other qualified health professional—such as a physical therapist, exercise physiologist, or nurse—is present and oversees the exercise. The following checklist will help you determine whether you should exercise under supervision.

✓   **Do I Need**   ✓
a Supervised Exercise Program?

If you meet any of the following conditions, you should play it safe and begin exercising in a supervised program for at least the first 12 weeks. For those of you with severe breathing problems, this on-site medical supervision may have to be continued indefinitely.

_____ I have COPD that causes Grade 3 breathlessness or worse.

_____ I have cor pulmonale.

_____ During my exercise stress test, one of the following happened: I developed hypoxemia (my blood-oxygen concentration fell significantly); I was unable to reach a maximal MET value of at least 5; or I couldn't get my heart rate above 85% of my age-predicted value (assuming I'm not taking beta blockers, which depress the heart rate).

_____ I use supplemental oxygen at rest or during exercise.

_____ I have another disease or condition that makes aerobics problematic because it predisposes me to exercise-related complications. Examples of such conditions are heart disease, severe arthritis, a stroke, peripheral vascular disease, severe kidney disease, diabetes, cancer, and extreme obesity.

For financial reasons, the current trend is toward allowing some patients who ideally should begin to exercise under the trained and watchful eye of a doctor to go it alone, following a *medically directed* program. This is an exercise program specially tailored for them by their doctor but conducted without a health professional present to oversee the exertion. The reasons for this trend are largely socioeconomic and have little to do with medicine. For one thing, only large communities tend to have medically supervised rehabilitation exercise programs, which, when they are available, are often expensive. And the programs aren't always scheduled at universally convenient times.

Granted, it's trends like this one that make our exercise rehabilitation book series a necessity. Still, if you meet any of the criteria just listed, I recommend that you begin your exercise under medical supervision, at least for the first 12 weeks, if at all possible. Such a program will help you acquire the skills you need to self-regulate your exercise prescription later when you are on your own. If 12 weeks in such a program is beyond your budget or impossible for some other reason, get involved for a shorter time. Even one medically supervised session is better than none at all.

To find a suitable pulmonary rehabilitation exercise program, ask your doctor or investigate what's offered at local hospitals, YMCAs and YWCAs, Jewish community centers, or private medical facilities. Often a local cardiac rehabilitation program is a good choice because it is aimed at patients, like you, with special medical needs. You might also want to contact the American Association of Cardiovascular and Pulmonary Rehabilitation (7611 Elmwood Ave. Suite #201, Middleton, WI 53562) at (608) 831-6989 for guidance or to purchase their comprehensive directory of nationwide rehabilitation programs.

EXERCISE SAFETY GUIDELINE 4

Ask your doctor if you need to use supplemental oxygen during exercise. And know the warning signs of hypoxemia.

Hypoxemia is a dangerous lack of oxygen in the blood. Clearly, if you're prone to hypoxemia when you're doing nothing more vigorous than sitting, you must get this condition under control before you even contemplate any exertion. The symptoms of resting hypoxemia include fatigue, drowsiness, apathy, inattentiveness, a delayed reaction time, and quick exhaustion when doing anything remotely strenuous.[6] It is diagnosed by measuring the oxygen content of blood taken from one of your arteries, often the one in your wrist used for taking your pulse. If you have this problem, the best solution is to take in extra oxygen from an ambulatory oxygen-supply device, perhaps for up to 20 hours a day.[7]

Anyone who needs extra oxygen while at rest will need it even more during exercise. Of course, some people get hypoxemia only when they do something strenuous, like exercise. It's almost impossible to guess which COPD patients have a tendency for this condition and which don't. So a simple diagnostic procedure called *oximetry** should be performed during your pretraining exercise test (this is especially important if your COPD causes Grade 3 breathlessness or worse) and during all exercise-related follow-up checkups.[8] Waiting to see if you develop hypoxemia symptoms during exercise isn't smart. The symptoms may include a lack of coordination and judgment, akin to being drunk from too much alcohol. But often there are no obvious symptoms.

Fortunately for those of you who need extra oxygen when you exercise, there are now lightweight, portable oxygen-supply systems.[9]

Symptoms of resting hypoxemia

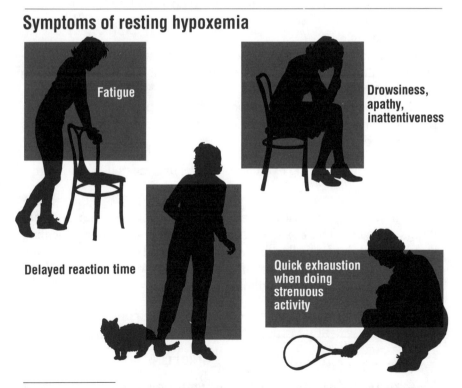

Fatigue

Drowsiness, apathy, inattentiveness

Delayed reaction time

Quick exhaustion when doing strenuous activity

*During oximetry, a special probe, connected to a computer, is attached to an earlobe or finger, enabling your doctor to obtain a continuous estimate of your blood-oxygen content while you're on a stationary cycle or treadmill or otherwise exerting yourself during an exercise test.

The oxygen can be delivered through your nose, mouth, or windpipe. The windpipe, or *transtracheal*, method is usually the most effective way to get oxygen into your lungs. Your doctor should give you explicit instructions on the use of supplemental oxygen during exercise and, if you are receiving transtracheal oxygen, on the correct technique for cleaning and changing the catheter.

EXERCISE SAFETY GUIDELINE 5

Be thoroughly versed in the warning signs of an impending cardiac complication.

By giving you this information on exercise safety, I don't mean to scare you away. Exercise is a much more normal state for the human body than inactivity, and most people with breathing problems can exercise safely.

What it comes down to is this: You're probably far more likely to die from the deleterious effects of sedentary living than you are to suffer from sudden death during exercise.

On the other hand, it's still prudent to keep your risk as low as possible. One of the best ways to boost your benefit-to-risk ratio is to remember this axiom:

Although death during exercise is always unexpected, it's seldom unheralded.

In other words, in many instances you'll have some warning that things are awry. The box that follows lists the bodily signs indicating that all might not be well with your heart. Should you experience any of them before, during, or just after an exercise session, discuss them with your doctor before continuing with exercise.

EXERCISE SAFETY GUIDELINE 6

Never disregard a worsening of your symptoms or the development of new ones.

WARNING SIGNS OF HEART PROBLEMS

- *Pain or discomfort in your chest, abdomen, back, neck, jaw, or arms.* Such symptoms may be signs of an inadequate supply of blood and oxygen to your heart muscle due to potentially serious conditions such as atherosclerotic plaque buildup in your coronary arteries.
- *Nausea during or after exercise.* This can result from a variety of causes, but it may signify a cardiac abnormality.
- *Unaccustomed shortness of breath during exercise.* People with a breathing disorder already have a problem with breathlessness. The operative word here is *unaccustomed.* If you ordinarily walk 2 miles in 45 minutes without extreme breathlessness and then one day you can't do it anymore, you should be alarmed. Although this may be related to your respiratory problems, it could also signal heart trouble.
- *Dizziness or fainting.* This can occur in healthy people who don't follow proper exercise protocol and fail to cool down adequately. Stopping exercise suddenly can cause anyone to feel momentarily dizzy or even to actually faint. I'm mainly concerned about dizziness that occurs while you're exercising rather than on stopping suddenly. This is a more probable sign of a serious problem—such as hypoxemia or heart trouble—and warrants immediate medical consultation.
- *An irregular pulse, particularly when it's been regular in past exercise sessions.* If you notice what appears to be extra heartbeats or skipped beats, notify your doctor. This, too, might not mean anything significant. On the other hand, it could point to heart problems.
- *A very rapid heart rate at rest.* If your heart rate is 100 beats per minute or higher after at least 5 minutes of rest, report this to your doctor. Although this could result from several causes, including some bronchodilator medications, it can also point to cardiac abnormalities.

The most accurate way to depict trends for better or worse in your condition is to compare the results of various sophisticated tests—such as pulmonary function and exercise tests and chest X rays—over time. But you also have an active role in monitoring your condition. It's up to you to pay close attention to any new signals or symptoms from your body. Here are some key ones that, in addition to those already discussed, indicate your condition could be worsening and that medical attention is required:

- Fever
- Coughing, wheezing, or breathlessness that is more frequent or severe than usual
- Increased sputum production or a change in its thickness or color
- Blood in the sputum
- Waking up more frequently at night to urinate
- Dehydration, as evidenced by dark urine and unusual dryness of the skin
- Sudden weight gain of more than 2 or 3 pounds
- Swelling of the ankles, legs, or abdomen

Of course, medication and appropriate exercise may, over time, improve your breathing problem or at least relieve some of the symptoms. You can monitor trends in your condition with a simple-to-use, inexpensive, small, portable device called a *peak-flow meter*. You blow into it, and it indicates the degree of your airflow obstruction. You can get one from your doctor or local pharmacy.

Your exercise training diary (see the end of chapter 3) can also reveal useful data over a period of months about changes in your heart rate and RPE or RPB ratings.

EXERCISE SAFETY GUIDELINE 7

Put safety at the top of your exercise priority list by following proper exercise protocol.

When it comes to exercise, there's a right way and a wrong way, a safe way and a dangerous way. As I mentioned previously, all exercisers—healthy or otherwise—should adhere to proper exercise protocol. The following elements of exercise protocol are especially relevant for exercisers with breathing problems.

- *Warm up and cool down for at least 5 minutes each.* Sufficient warm-up and cool-down are important for every exerciser because more than 70% of cardiac problems that surface during exercise do so either at the beginning or end of a session. Recent studies suggest that an adequate warm-up and cool-down are especially critical for people with COPD because their lungs, heart, and circulation require more time to adapt to changes in exertion levels.[10] This is particularly true for anyone who has undergone a single- or double-lung transplant or combined heart-lung transplant.[11,12]

- *Don't exercise in adverse hot-weather conditions, particularly without taking adequate precautions.* Hyperthermia—an overheating of the body during exercise—not only impairs your ability to exercise but also predisposes you to heatstroke, a potentially fatal condition. Moreover, the dehydration that usually accompanies hyperthermia can cause a thickening of your chest mucous secretions, thus worsening your airway obstruction. The symptoms of hyperthermia include headache, dizziness, confusion, stumbling, nausea, cramps, and cessation of sweating or excessive sweating.

To avoid hyperthermia, here are four preventive measures you can take:

- If you're exercising outdoors, let weather conditions guide the amount and intensity of exercise you should do on a given

Symptoms of hyperthermia

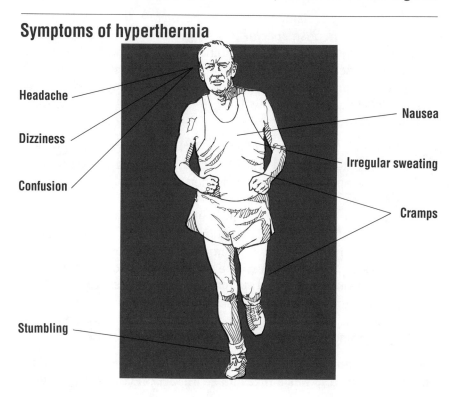

day. When heat and humidity are high, be sensible—don't engage in strenuous exercise.

- Drink fluids while you're exercising, especially on hot days. Do this even if you're not thirsty. About 15 minutes before you begin your session, drink about 8 ounces (240 milliliters) of cold water, which is absorbed more quickly than lukewarm. If your workout lasts longer than 30 minutes, take another 8-ounce drink at 15- to 20-minute intervals during exercise.

  Water may be the safest drink for you. If you have severe breathlessness during exercise, you probably do not want to drink beverages with a high-carbohydrate content because these may increase the body's ventilatory requirements.[13] Similarly, always wait 2 to 3 hours after eating a large meal before exercising.

- When exercising in warm weather, wear clothing that promotes heat loss. Fabrics that "breathe," such as a mesh or fishnet T-shirt, are good choices.

- If you must exercise in the heat, sponge off the exposed parts of your body with cool water at regular intervals.

- *If you're exercising outdoors, be aware that cold-weather exercise sessions pose special challenges and dangers for COPD patients.* Many people with breathing problems find that very cold air causes bronchospasm and a worsening of their airflow obstruction. Use good judgment about exercising in the cold. Stay indoors when the windchill index falls below 15 °F (–10 °C). Here are some other tips about cold-weather workouts:

  - Choose appropriate clothing. Select clothing that provides adequate insulation from the cold, but avoid fabrics that will cause an excessive sweat buildup. One answer is to dress in multiple layers of clothing.
  - Take longer to warm up than usual. An adequate warm-up is important under ideal conditions; it is crucial in cold weather.
  - Warm the air before it enters your lungs. You can do this by covering your mouth with a ski mask or a scarf. Or you can try to breathe through your nose as much as possible. Air is warmed more when it passes through the nasal passages than through the mouth. Both approaches—but especially nose breathing—are difficult during *strenuous* exercise.

- *Don't exercise in a polluted environment.* The quality of the air you breathe also has a measurable impact on your ability to work out safely. The U.S. Environmental Protection Agency singles out the following as the seven most common pollutants: total suspended particulates (for example, dust, soot, and pollen), sulfur dioxide, carbon monoxide, nitrogen dioxide, ozone, hydrocarbons, and lead. The major sources of these pollutants are vehicles, electric power plants that burn coal or oil, and factories (steel, metal, oil, and paper mills are the worst offenders).

The two pollutants that probably pose the most threat to people with breathing problems are carbon monoxide and ozone. Carbon monoxide, mostly contained in vehicle exhaust and cigarette smoke, interferes with the blood's ability to carry oxygen. Ozone, which is the result of a chemical reaction between automobile emissions and sunlight, irritates the lungs and worsens airflow obstruction.[14]

To avoid excessive carbon monoxide exposure, don't work out along heavily traveled roads at any time, especially during rush hour. Along roads with light traffic, try to stay at least 22 yards (20 meters) away from passing vehicles.

To avoid ozone, change your daily exercise schedule in the late spring and summer, when sunlight is strongest. During these seasons, try to exercise outdoors right at dawn or after the sun has set; ozone starts building up around 90 minutes after dawn and stops being generated at sunset. The peak ozone concentration is at midday.

• *Be cautious about high-altitude exercise.* At higher altitudes, expect to have a greater problem than usual with breathlessness. The decreased barometric pressure lessens your body's ability to filter oxygen out of the air. Even at moderate altitudes, expect your heart rate to be about 8% higher for a given exercise intensity than it is at sea level.[15]

Until you become acclimated to a higher altitude—which takes several weeks—it's wise to reduce the pace of your usual workout in order to stay within your designated heart rate, RPE, and RPB limits. For a while, you may also want to divide your exercise session into two or more shorter daily workouts.

• *Skip exercise when you have a fever, influenza, or other moderately serious acute illness.* You may not think it's necessary to include this warning. After all, who would want to exercise when sick? Believe it or not, lots of exercise enthusiasts I know.

Why are an infectious fever and aerobics a dubious combination? Exerting yourself heavily while you have an infection—including influenza—can trigger hyperthermia, worsen the infection, increase your predisposition for hypoxemia, and, sometimes, place you at risk for *viral myocarditis*, a potentially lethal inflammatory condition of the heart muscle.[16]

Acute illnesses usually subside on their own after a relatively short time or can be cured. If you've got nothing more serious than a slight cold, go ahead with aerobics if your temperature is normal, your symptoms are above your neck (for example, runny nose, sneezing, scratchy throat), and you feel like it. But when your acute ailment is more serious—and especially if it's accompanied by a fever—sit out aerobics and all other forms of strenuous exercise until you're better. After an illness, ease your way back into aerobics gradually over at least a week or two.

• *Wear quality shoes designed for the type of weight-bearing exercise you're doing.* Wearing the right shoes is crucial for anyone who wants to sidestep foot and knee problems and injuries. Thanks to technological advances, you can buy shoes that are specially designed for a particular sport and engineered to suit a specific foot type. Ask a member of your health-care team about what type of shoes meets your particular needs. Also, shop at a store where the sales staff is truly knowledgeable about athletic footgear. (You'll further reduce joint problems if you perform any high-impact, weight-bearing activity, such as jogging, on a soft surface rather than on a hard, nonresistant one. For example, choose grass over cement.)

EXERCISE SAFETY GUIDELINE 8

Be aware of how certain medications can alter your body's response to exercise.

If you've got COPD, it's likely you're on drug therapy. If you're elderly, you're probably taking medications for other chronic ailments as well. Some drugs greatly alter the body's response to exertion, so it's important to check with your doctor about this.

DRUG ALERT FOR BREATHING DISORDER PATIENTS

Ask your doctor if any medications you're taking place you at greater risk during exercise or modify your heart rate response.

Here are a few basic facts you should know about COPD drugs and exercise:

- Beta-agonist bronchodilator drugs—such as albuterol (e.g., Proventil, Ventolin), isoetharine (e.g., Bronkosol), metaproterenol (e.g., Alupent), and terbutaline (e.g., Brethine)—may increase your heart rate response to exercise even when they're administered in inhaler form.
- Theophylline (e.g., Choledyl, Theo-Dur), a xanthine-derivative bronchodilator drug, may not only boost your heart rate during exercise but also predispose you to potentially dangerous heart rhythm disturbances—especially when taken in too large a dose.[17,18] If you're taking this drug, your doctor should monitor its concentration in your blood at 6- to 12-month intervals, at the very least. The possible warning signals of theophylline toxicity include nausea, vomiting, stomach pain, diarrhea, insomnia, muscle twitching, palpitations, and an irregular pulse.
- Cromolyn sodium (e.g., Intal), corticosteroids, and ipratropium bromide (e.g., Atrovent) are other commonly used COPD drugs. They generally do not alter the heart rate response to exercise.[5]

EXERCISE SAFETY GUIDELINE 9

If you have COPD, learn special breathing techniques that help relieve breathlessness during exercise.

You may already be aware of the pursed-lip breathing technique. It was formally developed in the early 20th century to help people like you relieve and control breathlessness during exercise.

Here's how you do it: You inhale air as usual but exhale through your mouth with your lips pursed, as if you're about to kiss someone or whistle. This causes a smaller escape route for expelled air—through your pursed lips—and forces your body to maintain a higher lung pressure. This lung pressure helps prevent your smaller bronchial tubes from collapsing from too rapid an expulsion of air. Thus, your airways stay open longer, enabling more air to leave your lungs.

Of course, there are other breathing techniques, most of which involve better use of the diaphragm. Ask your pulmonary rehabilitation team about them.

EXERCISE SAFETY GUIDELINE 10

Know how to prevent, or at least minimize, exercise-induced asthma.

Exercise-induced asthma (EIA) is a type of episodic asthma. As such, it is reversible and is a far less severe breathing disorder than COPD. But it's significant because it affects about 80% of asthma patients, 40% of people with hay fever, and 12% to 15% of the general U.S. population![19]

It's well established that sustained, vigorous exertion, such as aerobic exercise, can trigger EIA. But its precise physiological genesis is still in dispute despite considerable research. The prevailing theory is that EIA results from bronchospasm—a condition in which the muscular walls of the bronchial tubes involuntarily contract and remain narrowed for 30 to 90 minutes. The attack ends either spontaneously or in response to an inhaled medication. The bronchospasm may also be accompanied by an inflammation and swelling of the inside lining of the bronchial tubes, which further restricts airflow.[20] EIA's major symptoms are wheezing, breathlessness, chest tightness, and coughing.

An EIA attack occurs either *during* a bout of vigorous exercise that lasts 6 to 12 minutes or longer or, more commonly, about 5 to 10 minutes *after you stop* such sustained exercise.[21] To diagnose EIA, your doctor will listen to your chest with a stethoscope and put you through pulmonary function tests, both before and after 6 to 12 minutes of vigorous exercise. Prescribing medication is something of a trial-and-error matter, however. To decide which drug, or combination of drugs, works best for you, your doctor will probably ask you to take the drug and then repeat the tests to see how your body reacts.

Under most circumstances, EIA is not life-threatening; the attack usually ends long before hospitalization or emergency resuscitation is necessary.[22] But it's a scary experience, one that, I'm sure, has deterred many people from regular exercise.

Whereas investigators may still be looking for EIA's precise mechanism, sports medicine authorities have taken the practical approach and focused instead on ways to insure that an attack never occurs in the first place. Their knowledge has helped scores of EIA-prone athletes continue to compete, excel, and even win world titles without worrying about the threat of an asthma episode disrupting their performance.

The next section provides a summary of important facts about EIA and how to prevent it. (For a more thorough discussion of EIA, see one of the several books devoted to the topic, such as *Asthma and Exercise* by Nancy Hogshead and Gerald Couzens.[23])

HELPFUL FACTS AND HINTS ABOUT EXERCISE-INDUCED ASTHMA AND ITS PREVENTION

If, in addition to EIA, you have any other forms of episodic asthma or chronic asthmatic bronchitis, first get those other conditions under control. This might only require avoiding other asthma triggers. Or it might call for taking medication. Once these other conditions are being properly treated and the airway inflammation they cause is controlled, the likelihood of EIA will diminish.

Some people with EIA can control it adequately by nonpharmacological means. However, this often limits exercise options, so most people usually take a drug as well. Discuss with your physician the possibility of controlling your EIA with medication. Here are some things you should know about EIA drugs:

- These drugs will only control your condition. They will not cure it. But in so doing, they'll enable you to participate in any sport or exercise on an equal footing with others.
- If a drug or combination of drugs is prescribed, ask your doctor for explicit instructions on how and when to use the medication. Specifically, you need to know how soon before you start exercise to take the medication, how long its action will last, and any side effects it tends to engender. (See Table 5.1 for information to use in discussions with your doctor.)
- Inhaled drugs are generally preferable to oral ones. They begin action in the body sooner, their effectiveness is superior, a lower dosage is necessary, and side effects are fewer.
- Even though beta-agonists (such as albuterol, metaproterenol, and terbutaline) are intended to prevent EIA (and may do so in 80% to 95% of persons), they also offer the most rapid relief from symptoms once an attack has begun. Always keep such an inhaler handy when exercising.

Table 5.1 summarizes how different types of medication are taken and their effects.

Table 5.1
Medication Useful for Preventing Exercise-Induced Asthma

Type of medication	Method of administration	How long before exercise medication should be taken (minutes)	Expected duration of beneficial effects (hours)
Beta-agonists			
Albuterol (e.g.,	Inhalation	15	4-6
Proventil, Ventolin)	Orally	30	4-6
Metaproterenol	Inhalation	10	2-4
(e.g., Alupent)	Orally	30	2-4
Terbutaline (e.g.,	Inhalation	15	3-6
Brethine)	Orally	30	4-6
Cromolyn sodium	Inhalation	10-20	4-6
(e.g., Intal)			
Theophylline (e.g.,	Orally	30-120	4-24
Choledyl, Theo-Dur)			
Anticholinergics	Inhalation	60	Unknown
Ipratropium bromide			
(e.g., Atrovent)			

Note. The values provided in this chart are intended as general guidelines and may vary in certain circumstances—check with your doctor to see if they are appropriate for you. Adapted from: R. Afrasiabi, S.L. Spector, "Exercise-Induced Asthma. It Needn't Sideline Your Patients." The Physician and Sportsmedicine 19 (1991): 49-62.

It's important to understand the *refractory period*, the time during which the threat of a follow-up EIA attack is greatly reduced. Once exercise has triggered an attack and you have stopped exercising to recover from it, you can return to exercise within the next hour—and possibly up to 4 hours later. During this period, another attack is unlikely, and if one does occur, it will be milder.

EIA is usually triggered by high-intensity exercise that lasts longer than 6 minutes.[24] You can reduce your chances of triggering an attack by doing one of the following:

• *Capitalize on the refractory period.* You don't need to have an initial EIA attack to do this. Here's how: Warm up for 10 minutes or so—some athletes with EIA stretch their warm-up to as long as 30 minutes—before you begin high-intensity exertion. The warm-up exercises needn't use the same muscles as you'll use during the higher intensity portion of your workout to cause a refractory period and lessen your risk for EIA.[25]

• *Exercise toward the lower end of your target heart rate zone.* In other words, exert yourself less strenuously but for a somewhat longer period.

• *Perform intermittent, higher intensity exercise in bouts of 30 to 60 seconds with short rests—or lower intensity exercise—in between.* Weight lifting and other muscle-strengthening exercises rarely trigger EIA because you rest in between.

Avoid working out in cold, dry air. EIA attacks are more likely in such air. EIA is thought to be caused by the release of special chemical substances in response to heat and water loss from the airways during the warming and humidifying of large amounts of inhaled air. If you must work out in such an environment, breathe through a face mask or scarf placed over your mouth, or breathe only through your nose. Doing the latter will mean limiting yourself to very low intensity exercise, though.

Avoid working out in polluted environments, another potential trigger of EIA. Pollution, in this instance, includes toxic substances (such as those discussed under Guideline 7), pollen, and other airborne irritants that you may be allergic to. But don't go to the extreme of moving to another part of the country. Remember the old saying, "Better the devil you know than one you don't." Although you may leave behind old triggers, your new home may have its own set of unexpected triggers.

Be aware that some exercises are more likely to cause EIA than others. The following are listed in order from those most to least likely to trigger an attack: outdoor running, treadmill running, cycling, walking, and pool swimming.[26] Pool swimming has a low tendency to induce asthma because it is accompanied by the inhalation of the warm, moist air hovering just above the surface of the water. The recommended pool temperature for swimmers with EIA is around 86 °F (30 °C).

Make sure your cool-down is adequate. EIA typically occurs after exercise, so prolonging the low-intensity exertion at the end of your workout will help stave off an attack. So, too, may taking a warm shower or bath and breathing the warm, moist air and then changing into warm clothing.[27]

SOME CONCLUDING THOUGHTS

In this book, I've offered you a state-of-the-art method for using regular exercise to reduce your breathlessness and optimize both the quality and quantity of your life. My advice has been based on what is currently known about exercise and breathing disorders. In the years to come, more will be learned about how patients with respiratory ailments, such as yourself, can derive the most from an exercise rehabilitation program. But don't wait until then to begin a physically active lifestyle. Now is the time for you, in consultation with your doctor, to formulate your specific exercise plan from the blueprint I've provided.

The sooner you begin a sensible exercise program, the sooner you will reap the many rewards. Once you do get started, never forget that exercise should be fun. I've always thoroughly enjoyed it and have no doubt that with time you will, too.

Good luck! And the best of health to you.

Chapter 5
Prescription

- ❑ Don't contemplate exercise until your breathing problem has been stabilized through appropriate medical treatment.
- ❑ Have a thorough medical evaluation before starting your exercise program—and at regular intervals thereafter.
- ❑ Find out whether you need direct medical supervision when you exercise—and for what period of time.
- ❑ Ask your doctor if you need to use supplemental oxygen during exercise.
- ❑ If you have chronic bronchitis or emphysema, know the warning signs of hypoxemia, a dangerous lack of oxygen in the blood.
- ❑ Be thoroughly versed in the warning signs of an impending cardiac complication.
- ❑ Never disregard a worsening of your symptoms or the development of new ones.
- ❑ Don't exercise in adverse climatic conditions, particularly without taking adequate precautions.
- ❑ Don't exercise in a polluted environment.
- ❑ Be cautious about high-altitude exercise.
- ❑ Skip exercise when you have a fever, influenza, or other moderately serious acute illness.
- ❑ Wear quality shoes designed for the specific type of weight-bearing exercise you are doing.
- ❑ Be aware of how medications can alter your body's response to exercise. Ask your doctor if you're taking any medications that require special precautions during exercise.
- ❑ If you have COPD, learn special breathing techniques that can help relieve breathlessness during exercise.
- ❑ Know how to prevent, or at least minimize, exercise-induced asthma.
- ❑ Don't perform too much exercise too early in your program.

Appendix A

How to Take Your Pulse and Calculate Your Heart Rate

Y ou have two pulse points to choose from—the radial artery in your wrist or the carotid artery in your throat (see Figure A.1). Your radial artery is the preferred place because the reading there is usually more accurate.

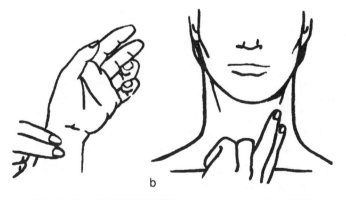

a   b

Figure A.1 Pulse points: a) radial artery, b) carotid artery. *Note.* From *ACSM Fitness Book* (p. 24) by The American College of Sports Medicine, 1992, Champaign, IL: Leisure Press. Copyright 1992 by The American College of Sports Medicine. Reprinted by permission.

Your two carotid arteries are located on either side of your windpipe. These arteries are large, and you should be able to locate them easily by gently pressing just to the right or left of your Adam's apple. But there are several things you must keep in mind. Don't press hard; press on only one carotid artery at a time; and do not press too near the jawbone. If you do any of these things your heart rate may slow down excessively and result in potentially harmful consequences, not to mention an inaccurate reading.

Taking your pulse is a three-step process. Here are instructions for taking a wrist pulse reading. Resort to your carotid artery only if you absolutely cannot locate the radial artery in your wrist.

1. *Locate the pulse in your wrist.* The hand of your wristwatch arm is the one you will use to monitor the pulse in your opposite wrist. Your "sensors" are the pads of your fingers, not your fingertips.

Place your index finger and middle finger at the base of the outer third of your wrist, the side on which your thumb is located. If you feel your wrist's tendons, you need to move your fingers further to the outside of your wrist. Do this incrementally, changing the location of your fingers by about a quarter of an inch until you finally locate a pulsation. Don't press too hard or you may obliterate your pulse. A light but firm pressure is all that is needed. You should be able to feel your pulse each time your heart beats, thus making your pulse rate equivalent to your heart rate.

2. *Count your pulse.* To determine your *resting heart rate*, count for 30 to 60 seconds. Your heart rate varies with your breathing; it slows down when you exhale and speeds up when you inhale. Thus if you count your pulse for shorter periods, you won't get a good average reading.

Taking a reading during exercise is different. Then your pulse rate is faster so a 10-second count is sufficient. If you're exercising in a stationary position—on a cycle ergometer, for example—you can count your pulse easily without stopping. However, if you're moving—such as walking or jogging—you'll need to stop, but not completely. Keep your legs moving while you take your pulse, which *you must do immediately.* If you wait for more than a second or two, your heart starts to slow down. This is true particularly if you are fit. If you count for longer than 10 seconds, you run the risk of greatly *underestimating* your heart rate.

When counting your pulse, count as "one" the first pulsation you feel *after* your watchhand hits a digit. Do *not* count as "one" any pulsation that occurs at the same time as the hand hits the digit.

Continue the count until your watch registers 10 seconds. If a pulsation occurs at the same time as the watchhand hits the 10-second point, count it, but none thereafter.

3. *Calculate your heart rate.* After you've counted your pulse for 10 seconds, multiply that number by 6 to get your heart rate (beats per minute). Here's a chart with the calculations already done for 10-second pulse counts of 12 through 31:

12 = 72	17 = 102	22 = 132	27 = 162
13 = 78	18 = 108	23 = 138	28 = 168
14 = 84	19 = 114	24 = 144	29 = 174
15 = 90	20 = 120	25 = 150	30 = 180
16 = 96	21 = 126	26 = 156	31 = 186

Appendix B

Tests and Procedures Included in a Thorough Pre-Exercise Medical Exam

H ere's a checklist of what's included in a thorough, state-of-the-art medical exam. Your checkup may not be as comprehensive if the equipment isn't available or if your medical history indicates that your case simply doesn't warrant it.

✓ **Checkup Checklist** ✓

_____ My physician or physician assistant takes a thorough medical history. He or she asks about diseases that I know I have, any symptoms suggestive of disease, and all medications I'm currently taking. We also discuss my breathing problems and my ability to perform the physical activities of daily living without undue breathlessness. Finally, the interviewer should ask about my attitudes toward exercise.

_____ I'm examined to assess the current status of my breathing disorder and of any other chronic diseases I may have that make exercise problematic. In particular, I'm given a thorough respiratory and cardiovascular exam, which includes the following:

_____ Blood pressure measurement while I'm lying down, sitting, and standing.

_____ Monitoring of the pulses in my neck, arms, and legs.

_____ Listening to my neck, chest, heart, abdomen, and femoral arteries in my groin with a stethoscope.

_____ Inspection of the veins in my neck, examination of my abdomen, and inspection of my ankles and legs for evidence of heart failure.

_____ If they've not been done recently, all of the following:

- a blood-lipid profile that goes much further than a mere total cholesterol count;
- a complete blood count and blood biochemistry profile;
- a chest X ray; and
- pulmonary function tests and arterial blood gas determinations (at the discretion of my doctor).

_____ A resting electrocardiogram (ECG).

_____ A treadmill or cycle ergometer exercise test (known as a symptom-limited maximal exercise test) with ECG and blood-pressure monitoring. The purpose is to evaluate my respiratory and cardiovascular response to exercise and to measure my aerobic fitness level. My doctor will listen to my chest before and after this test to determine whether exercise worsens my airflow obstruction. Using scales like those in chapter 3, I'll be asked to rate my effort or breathlessness during the test. If I have COPD—especially if it's severe enough to cause Grade 3 or greater breathlessness—I should be screened for exercise-induced hypoxemia with an oximetry device. If I experience exercise-induced asthma, pulmonary function tests should be done before and after exercise; I should also have these tests after taking various medications. Other more sophisticated measures, such as monitoring the air I exhale during exercise, may also be included.

_____ I'm checked out for any musculoskeletal problems that may limit my ability to exercise or be worsened by inappropriate exercise.

_____ My current strength and joint flexibility are measured, with or without sophisticated equipment.

_____ My body weight and, if possible, percentage body fat are measured.

_____ My doctor reviews the results of all pertinent previous tests and compares them to current results to ascertain trends in my health status.

_____ My physician uses his or her judgment in deciding what additional tests I need, given my circumstances.

Notes

FOREWORD

[1]Hodgkin, J.E. "Chronic Obstructive Pulmonary Disease: Preface." *Clinics in Chest Medicine* 11 (1990): ix-x.

[2]Higgins, M.W. "Chronic Airways Disease in the United States: Trends and Determinants." *Chest* 96 (1989): 328S-334S.

CHAPTER 1

[1]McCarthy, P. "Wheezing or Breezing Through Exercise-Induced Asthma." *Physician and Sportsmedicine* 17 (1989): 125-130.

[2]Cooper, K., and Cooper, M. *The New Aerobics for Women.* New York: Bantam Books, 1988.

[3]Sorvino, P. *How to Become a Former Asthmatic.* New York: William Morrow & Co., 1985.

[4]Comroe, J.H. "Some Theories of the Mechanism of Dyspnea." In *Breathlessness*, edited by J.B. Howell and E.J.M. Campbell. Boston: Blackwell Scientific Publications, Inc., 1966, pp. 1-7.

[5]Petty, T.L. "Definitions in Chronic Obstructive Pulmonary Disease." *Clinics in Chest Medicine* 11 (1990): 363-373.

[6]Ries, A.L. "Position Paper of the American Association of Cardiovascular and Pulmonary Rehabilitation: Scientific Basis of Pulmonary Rehabilitation." *Journal of Cardiopulmonary Rehabilitation* 10 (1990): 418-441.

[7]American Thoracic Society. "Pulmonary Rehabilitation: Official American Thoracic Society Position Statement." *American Review of Respiratory Diseases* 124 (1981): 663-666.

[8]Hodgkin, J.E. "Pulmonary Rehabilitation: Structure, Components and Benefits." *Journal of Cardiopulmonary Rehabilitation* 11 (1988): 423-434.

[9]American Association of Cardiovascular and Pulmonary Rehabilitation. *Guidelines for Pulmonary Rehabilitation Programs.* Champaign, IL: Human Kinetics, 1993.

CHAPTER 2

[1]Carter, R., et al. "Exercise Conditioning in the Rehabilitation of Patients with Chronic Obstructive Pulmonary Disease." *Archives of Physical Medicine and Rehabilitation* 69 (1988): 118-122.

[2]Leon, A.S., et al. "Leisure-Time Physical Activity Levels and Risk of Coronary Heart Disease and Death." *Journal of the American Medical Association* 258 (1987): 2388-2395.

[3]Adams, F., trans.-ed. *The Extant Works of Aretaeus the Cappadocian.* London: Sydenham Society, 1856.

[4]Bouchard, C., et al., eds. *Exercise, Fitness, and Health: A Consensus of Current Knowledge.* Champaign, IL: Human Kinetics, 1990.

[5]Ries, A.L. "Position Paper of the American Association of Cardiovascular and Pulmonary Rehabilitation: Scientific Basis of Pulmonary Rehabilitation." *Journal of Cardiopulmonary Rehabilitation* 10 (1990): 418-441.

[6]Hodgkin, J.E. "Pulmonary Rehabilitation." *Clinics in Chest Medicine* 11 (1990): 447-460.

[7]Jones, N.L. "Exercise in Chronic Airway Obstruction." In *Current Therapy in Sports Medicine—2*, edited by J.S. Torg et al. Toronto: B.C. Decker, Inc., 1990, pp. 31-34.

[8]Belman, M.J. "Exercise in Chronic Obstructive Pulmonary Disease." In *Exercise in Modern Medicine*, edited by B.A. Franklin et al. Baltimore: Williams & Wilkins, 1989, pp. 175-191.

[9]Cockcroft, A. "Pulmonary Rehabilitation." *British Journal of Diseases of the Chest* 82 (1988): 220-225.

[10]Saltin, B. "Cardiovascular and Pulmonary Adaptation to Physical Activity." In *Exercise, Fitness, and Health: A Consensus of Current Knowledge*, edited by C. Bouchard et al. Champaign, IL: Human Kinetics, 1990, pp. 187-203.

[11]Wasserman, K. "Dyspnea on Exertion: Is It the Heart or the Lungs?" *Journal of the American Medical Association* 248 (1982): 2039-2043.

[12]Casaburi, R., et al. "A New Perspective on Pulmonary Rehabilitation: Anaerobic Threshold as a Discriminant in Training." *European Respiratory Journal* 2 (1989): 618S-623S.

[13]Jones, N.L., et al. "Chronic Obstructive Respiratory Disorders." In *Exercise Testing and Exercise Prescription for Special Cases*, edited by J.S. Skinner. Philadelphia: Lea & Febiger, 1987, pp. 175-187.

[14]Haas, A., and Cardon, H. "Rehabilitation in Chronic Obstructive Pulmonary Disease: A 5-Year Study of 252 Male Patients." *Medical Clinics of North America* 53 (1969): 593-606.

[15]Lustig, F.M., Haas, A., and Castillo, R. "Clinical and Rehabilitation Regime in Patients with Chronic Obstructive Pulmonary Disease." *Archives of Physical Medicine and Rehabilitation* 53 (1972): 315-322.

[16]American College of Sports Medicine. *Guidelines for Exercise Testing and Prescription*. Philadelphia: Lea & Febiger, 1991.

[17]Powell, K.E., et al. "Physical Activity and the Incidence of Coronary Heart Disease." *Annual Review of Public Health* 8 (1987): 253-287.

[18]Berlin, G.A., and Colditz, G.A. "A Meta-Analysis of Physical Activity in the Prevention of Coronary Heart Disease." *American Journal of Epidemiology* 132 (1990): 612-628.

[19]Sidney, K.H., and Jerome, W.C. "Anxiety and Depression: Exercise for Mood Enhancement." In *Current Therapy in Sports Medicine—2*, edited by J.S. Torg et al. Toronto: B.C. Decker, Inc., 1990, pp. 159-165.

[20]Thoren, P., et al. "Endorphins and Exercise: Physiological Mechanisms and Clinical Implications." *Medicine and Science in Sports and Exercise* 22 (1990): 417-428.

[21]Holden, D.A., et al. "The Impact of a Rehabilitation Program on Functional Status in Patients With Chronic Lung Disease." *Respiratory Care* 35 (1990): 332-341.

[22]Hodgkin, J.E. "Chronic Obstructive Pulmonary Disease: Preface." *Clinics in Chest Medicine* 11 (1990): ix-x.

[23]Hodgkin, J.E. "Pulmonary Rehabilitation: Structure, Components, and Benefits." *Journal of Cardiopulmonary Rehabilitation* 11 (1988): 423-434.

[24]Cheong, R.H., et al. "Cardiac Arrhythmias During Exercise in Severe Chronic Pulmonary Disease." *Chest* 97 (1990): 793-797.

[25]Van Camp, S.P., and Peterson, R.A. "Cardiovascular Complications of Outpatient Cardiac Rehabilitation Programs." *Journal of the American Medical Association* 256 (1986): 1160-1163.

[26]Banner, N.R., et al. "Cardiopulmonary Response to Dynamic Exercise After Heart and Combined Heart-Lung Transplantation." *British Heart Journal* 61 (1989): 215-223.

[27]Miyoshi, S., et al. "Cardiopulmonary Exercise Testing After Single and Double Lung Transplantation." *Chest* 97 (1990): 1130-1136.

[28]Palevsky, H.I., and Fishman, A.P. "Chronic Cor Pulmonale: Etiology and Management." *Journal of the American Medical Association* 263 (1990): 2347-2353.

[29]Petty, T.L. "Home Oxygen: A Revolution in the Care of Advanced COPD." *Medical Clinics of North America* 74 (1990): 715-729.

[30]Macera, C., et al. "Predicting Lower-Extremity Injuries Among Habitual Runners." *Archives of Internal Medicine* 149 (1989): 2565-2568.

[31]Walter, S., et al. "The Ontario Cohort Study of Running-Related Injuries." *Archives of Internal Medicine* 149 (1989): 2561-2564.

[32]Blair, S.N., Kohl, H.W., and Goodyear, N.N. "Rates and Risks for Running and Exercise Injuries: Studies in Three Populations." *Research Quarterly for Exercise and Sport* 58 (1987): 221-228.

CHAPTER 3

[1]Institute for Aerobics Research. *The Strength Connection*. Dallas: Institute for Aerobics Research, 1990.

[2]Jones, N.L., and Killian, K.J. "Exercise in Chronic Airway Obstruction." In *Exercise, Fitness, and Health: A Consensus of Current Knowledge*, edited by C. Bouchard et al. Champaign, IL: Human Kinetics, 1990, pp. 547-559.

[3]Criner, G.J., and Celli, B.R. "Effects of Unsupported Arm Exercise on Ventilatory Muscle Recruitment in Patients With Severe Chronic Airflow Obstruction." *American Review of Respiratory Diseases* 138 (1988): 856-861.

[4]Mahler, D.A., and O'Donnell, D.E. "Alternative Modes of Exercise Training for Pulmonary Patients." *Journal of Cardiopulmonary Rehabilitation* 11 (1991): 58-63.

[5]Fraley Stratton, B. "Pulmonary Rehabilitation: For the Breath of Your Life." *Journal of Cardiopulmonary Rehabilitation* 9 (1989): 80-86.

[6]Hara, W.J., et al. "Weight Training Benefits in COPD: A Controlled Crossover Study." *Respiratory Care* 32 (1987): 660-668.

[7]Agre, J.C., et al. "Light Resistance and Stretching Exercise in Elderly Women: Effect Upon Strength." *Archives of Physical Medicine and Rehabilitation* 69 (1988): 273-276.

[8]Gordon, N.F., and Gibbons, L.W. *The Cooper Clinic Cardiac Rehabilitation Program*. New York: Simon & Schuster, 1990.

[9]Cooper, K.H. *Aerobics*. New York: Bantam Books, 1968.

[10]Blair, S.N., et al. "Exercise and Fitness in Childhood: Implications for a Lifetime of Health." In *Perspective in Exercise Science and Sports Medicine—2: Youth, Exercise and Sport*, edited by C.V. Gisolfi and D.R. Lamb. Indianapolis: Benchmark Press, 1989, pp. 401-430.

[11]American Heart Association. "Exercise Standards: A Statement for Health Professionals From the American Heart Association." *Circulation* 82 (1990): 2286-2322.

[12]Haskell, W.L., Montoye, H.J., and Orenstein, D. "Physical Activity and Exercise to Achieve Health-Related Physical Fitness Components." *Public Health Reports* 100 (1985): 202-212.

[13]Blair, S.N. *Living With Exercise*. Dallas: American Health Publishing Co., 1991.

[14]DeBusk, R.F., et al. "Training Effects of Long Versus Short Bouts of Exercise in Healthy Subjects." *American Journal of Cardiology* 65 (1990): 1010-1013.

[15]Reiff, D.B., et al. "The Effect of Prolonged Submaximal Warm-Up Exercise on Exercise-Induced Asthma." *American Review of Respiratory Diseases* 139 (1989): 479-484.

[16]American College of Sports Medicine. *Guidelines for Exercise Testing and Prescription*. Philadelphia: Lea & Febiger, 1991.

[17]Wilson, P.K., Bell, C.W., and Norton, A.C. *Rehabilitation of the Heart and Lungs*. Anaheim, CA: Sensormedics, 1985.

[18]Ries, A.L., and Archibald, C.J. "Endurance Exercise Training at Maximal Targets in Patients With Chronic Obstructive Pulmonary Disease." *Journal of Cardiopulmonary Rehabilitation* 7 (1987): 594-601.

[19]Carter, R.C., et al. "Exercise Conditioning in the Rehabilitation of Patients With Chronic Obstructive Pulmonary Disease." *Archives of Physical Medicine and Rehabilitation* 69 (1988): 118-122.

[20]Borg, G.A. "Psychophysical Bases of Perceived Exertion." *Medicine and Science in Sports and Exercise* 14 (1982): 377-387.

[21]Jones, N.L., et al. "Chronic Obstructive Respiratory Disorders." In *Exercise Testing and Exercise Prescription for Special Cases*, edited by J.S. Skinner. Philadelphia: Lea & Febiger, 1987, pp. 175-187.

[22]Belman, M.J. "Exercise in Chronic Obstructive Pulmonary Diseases." In *Exercise in Modern Medicine*, edited by B.A. Franklin et al. Baltimore: Williams & Wilkins, 1989, pp. 175-191.

[23]Thomas, T.R., and Londeree, B.R. "Energy Cost During Prolonged Walking vs. Jogging Exercise." *Physician and Sportsmedicine* 17 (1989): 93-102.

[24]Sharkey, B.J. "Specificity of Exercise." In *Resource Manual for Guidelines for Exercise Testing and Prescription*, edited by S.N. Blair et al. Philadelphia: Lea & Febiger, 1988, pp. 55-61.

[25]Yanker, G., and Burton, K. *Walking Medicine*. New York: McGraw-Hill, 1990.

[26]Katz, R.M. "Coping With Exercise-Induced Asthma in Sports." *Physician and Sportsmedicine* 15 (1987): 101-108.

CHAPTER 4

[1]Cooper, K.H. *The Aerobics Program for Total Well-Being*. New York: Bantam Books, 1982.

[2]Katz, R.M. "Coping With Exercise-Induced Asthma in Sports." *Physician and Sportsmedicine* 15 (1987): 101-108.

[3]Gwinup, G. "Weight Loss Without Dietary Restriction: Efficacy of Different Forms of Aerobic Exercise." *American Journal of Sports Medicine* 15 (1987): 275-279.

[4]Cooper, K.H. *Overcoming Hypertension*. New York: Bantam Books, 1990.

[5]McCarthy, P. "Wheezing or Breezing Through Exercise-Induced Asthma." *Physician and Sportsmedicine* 17 (1989): 125-130.

[6]DeBenedette, V. "Stair Machines: The Truth About This Fitness Fad." *Physician and Sportsmedicine* 18 (1990): 131-134.

[7]Williams, C., and Gordon, N. "Bench Stepping: An At-Home Introduction to the Hottest Trend in Aerobics." *Shape.* April 1990: 96-101.

[8]Gordon, N.F., et al. "Effects of Rest Interval Duration on Cardiorespiratory Responses to Hydraulic Resistance Circuit Training." *Journal of Cardiopulmonary Rehabilitation* 9 (1989): 325-330.

[9]Paffenbarger, R.S., Jr., et al. "Physical Activity, All-Cause Mortality, and Longevity in College Alumni." *New England Journal of Medicine* 314 (1986): 605-613.

[10]Coyle, E.F. "Detraining and Retention of Training-Induced Adaptations." In *Resource Manual for Guidelines for Exercise Testing and Prescription*, edited by S.N. Blair et al. Philadelphia: Lea & Febiger, 1988, pp. 83-89.

CHAPTER 5

[1]Cooper, K.H. *Running Without Fear.* New York: M. Evans & Co., 1985.

[2]Cooper, K.H. *The Aerobics Program for Total Well-Being.* New York: Bantam Books, 1982.

[3]Cooper, K.H., and Cooper, M. *The New Aerobics for Women.* New York: Bantam Books, 1988.

[4]Cockcroft, A. "Pulmonary Rehabilitation." *British Journal of Diseases of the Chest* 82 (1988): 220-225.

[5]American College of Sports Medicine. *Guidelines for Exercise Testing and Prescription.* Philadelphia: Lea & Febiger, 1991.

[6]Braunwald, E., et al., eds. *Harrison's Principles of Internal Medicine* 11th ed. New York: McGraw-Hill, 1987.

[7]Petty, T.L., and O'Donohue, W.G. "Ambulatory Oxygen: The Standard of Care." *Chest* 98 (1990): 791-792.

[8]Belman, M.J. "Exercise in Chronic Obstructive Pulmonary Disease." In *Exercise in Modern Medicine*, edited by B.A. Franklin et al. Baltimore: Williams & Wilkins, 1989, pp. 175-191.

[9]Petty, T.L. "Home Oxygen: A Revolution in the Care of Advanced COPD." *Medical Clinics of North America* 74 (1990): 715-729.

[10]Chick, T.W., et al. "Recovery of Gas Exchange Variables After Maximal Exercise in COPD." *Chest* 97 (1990): 276-279.

[11]Miyoshi, S., Trulock, E.P., and Schaef, H.J. "Cardiopulmonary Exercise Testing After Single and Double Lung Transplantation." *Chest* 97 (1990): 1130-1136.

[12]Kimoff, R.J., et al. "Pulmonary Denervation in Humans." *American Review of Respiratory Diseases* 142 (1990): 1034-1040.

[13]Sklarek, H., et al. "Effect of High and Low Carbohydrate Nutritional Supplementation on Exercise Performance in COPD." *American Review of Respiratory Diseases* 135 (1987): A359.

[14]Horstman, D.H., et al. "Ozone Concentration and Pulmonary Response Relationships for 6.6-Hour Exposures With Five Hours of Moderate Exercise to 0.08, 0.10, and 0.12 ppm." *American Review of Respiratory Diseases* 142 (1990): 1158-1163.

[15]Squires, R.W. "Moderate Altitude Exposure and the Cardiac Patient." *Journal of Cardiopulmonary Rehabilitation* 5 (1985): 421-426.

[16]Ilback, N.G., Fohlman, J., and Friman, G. "Exercise in Coxsackie B3 Myocarditis: Effects on Heart Lymphocyte Subpopulations and the Inflammatory Reaction." *American Heart Journal* 117 (1989): 1298-1302.

[17]Sessler, C.N., and Cohen, M.D. "Cardiac Arrhythmias During Theophylline Toxicity." *Chest* 98 (1990): 672-678.

[18]Bittar, G., and Friedman, H.S. "The Arrhythmogencity of Theophylline." *Chest* 99 (1991): 1415-1420.

[19]Afrasiabi, R., and Spector, S.L. "Exercise-Induced Asthma: It Needn't Sideline Your Patients." *Physician and Sportsmedicine* 19 (1991): 49-62.

[20]McFadden, E.R., Jr. "Hypothesis: Exercise-Induced Asthma as a Vascular Phenomenon." *Lancet* 335 (1990): 880-883.

[21]Katz, R.M. "Coping With Exercise-Induced Asthma in Sports." *Physician and Sportsmedicine* 15 (1987): 101-108.

[22]McFadden, E.R., Jr. "Exercise and Asthma." *New England Journal of Medicine* 317 (1987): 502-504.

[23]Hogshead, N., and Couzens, G.C. *Asthma and Exercise*. New York: Henry Holt & Co., 1990.

[24]Nickerson, B.G. "Asthmatic Patients and Those With Exercise-Induced Bronchospasm." In *Exercise in Modern Medicine*, edited by B.A. Franklin et al. Baltimore: Williams & Wilkins, 1989, pp. 192-203.

[25]Reiff, D.B., et al. "The Effect of Prolonged Submaximal Warm-Up Exercise on Exercise-Induced Asthma." *American Review of Respiratory Diseases* 139 (1989): 479-484.

[26]Wilson, B.A., Bar-Or, O., and Seed, L.G. "Effects of Humid Air Breathing During Arm or Treadmill Exercise on Exercise-Induced Bronchoconstriction and Refractoriness." *American Review of Respiratory Diseases* 142 (1990): 349-352.

[27]Morton, A.R., and Fitch, K.D. "Exercise-Induced Bronchial Obstruction." In *Current Therapy in Sports Medicine—2*, edited by J.S. Torg et al. Toronto: B.C. Decker, Inc., 1990, pp. 53-59.

Index